PELICAN BOOKS

A952

GOD IS NO MORE

Werner Pelz was born in Berlin of Jewish parents, and Lotte, his wife, was born in Vienna. They came to England just before the war and 'passed through a variety of emotional and professional vicissitudes' both before and after they met and married in Oxford. They write: 'Encouraged in our quixotism by the poetic insights of the Old and New Testament, we drifted into and out of the church in our endeavours to recapture and communicate them. Today – free, and neither within nor without church or -ism – a grant enables us to delve into our inheritance and to share our enthralling discoveries – enthralling at least to us – with others. Our hobby is living, including much between Bach and Picasso, Homer and Nietzsche, Leviathan and the honey fly. We love writing plays, unclassifiable fiction and short stories.'

They are the authors of three books: *Distant Strains of Triumph* ('a kind of autobiography'), *God Is No More*, and *True Deceivers*, and they have contributed to *The God I Want* (1967).

Werner and Lotte Pelz have a son and now live in Wales.

WERNER AND LOTTE PELZ

God is No More

WITH A FOREWORD
BY EDWARD CARPENTER
CANON OF WESTMINSTER

If Thou humblest Thyself, Thou humblest Me.
Thou also dwell'st in Eternity.
Thou art a Man: God is no more:
Thy own Humanity learn to adore,
For that is My spirit of life.

                                        BLAKE

PENGUIN BOOKS

Penguin Books Ltd, Harmondsworth, Middlesex, England
Penguin Books Australia Ltd, Ringwood, Victoria, Australia

—

First published by Victor Gollancz 1963
Published in Pelican Books 1968

—

Copyright © Werner and Lotte Pelz, 1963

—

Made and printed in Great Britain by
C. Nicholls & Company Ltd
Set in Monotype Garamond

Contents

Authors' Recommendation

OUR notes as well as our biblical references often represent an integral part of our argument. We never use a Bible text to prove anything. We rarely use it simply as an illustration. We frequently try to establish between our interpretation and the quotation that dialectical tension which can become a source of cross-illumination, throwing light both on the text quoted and on our comment. We should, therefore, be most grateful to our reader – and hope that he, in turn, will feel grateful to us – if he would take the trouble of looking up our references, especially if he is not very familiar with the New Testament – or too familiar.

Foreword

EVERY now and again, from the arid waste lands of much contemporary 'religious' literature, there comes a book which provokes, excites and compels. It does so because it embodies a living and vital experience which breaks through and refuses to be contained by the language which holds it.

Such a book is *God Is No More* by Werner and Lotte Pelz. Here the printed page represents the struggle to express the inexpressible: it is the projection of a deep inner conflict which moves in a world of both annihilation and fulfilment. The authors would surely have agreed with F. D. Maurice that 'the systematizer is of the devil'. For this reason *God Is No More* endeavours to escape from the prison house of formal statement, to be free of precise categories, and to be true to the deeps of more primal yet ultimate experience. 'Words are the wise men's counters; they do but reckon by them. But they are the money of fools.' So wrote Thomas Hobbes. God is no more because He has become an idea – a mere word; and this has confined Him within neat and tidy systems. He is found at the end of an argument; His nature is formally stated; He is conventionalized, made familiar and respectable – and so He dies.

Werner and Lotte Pelz will have none of these things: and they refuse them because their own experience cannot be so categorized; cannot be stated, but only externalized. The living stuff of what has happened in them is too concrete and particular to allow it to be theoretically formulated in terms of general principles. The words of Jesus become relevant because they meet the Pelzs' situation, and the resulting life-death encounter brings with it an infinite promise, which is such as to validate the truth of the words, indeed which creates their truth. The authority of the words of Jesus – if any, the authors write, resides in themselves. Unless they convince and convict me, nothing in heaven and earth can compel me to accept them, or convince me of their truth or usefulness – certainly not a belief that Jesus was 'God' or the 'Son of God'. This is their freedom and their power. Where they have been heard as they want to be heard, they awaken a desire and a hope which find their expression in the belief that he who speaks them *lives*. But: *I do not believe in the truth of the words of Jesus because I believe that he lives. I believe he lives when I am persuaded to believe in the truth of his words.*

So would Werner and Lotte Pelz affirm, of the words of Jesus, as the author of the Epistle to the Hebrews affirmed of the Word of God, that they are 'quick and powerful, and sharper than any two edged sword, piercing even to the dividing asunder of soul and spirit, and of the joints and marrow'. They become so, however, because they speak to, and at the same time evoke, an already felt experience. The result is that the Pelzs' interpretation of these words is shot through with a penetrating insight. Gone are the pious phrases and threadbare platitudes which reduce the sayings of Jesus to the precision and exactitude of an A.B.C. railway guide. Indeed the insight often sheds light by the sheer novelty of the explication, particularly in the case of an utterance which has been robbed of vitality by familiarity or a traditional interpretation. The reader may often think that the explanation is so individual, so paradoxical, often so highly selective, as to become precarious. It is just here that its strength lies, though the criticism may still be a true one. The very 'openness' of this book; the refusal by the authors to restrict man's spirit to the confines of any religious law; the willingness to shed the false security of external authority for trust in an inner self-validating constraint, these constitute a liberation. Faith has to emerge out of doubt, hope out of despair and life out of death. It is Jesus who refuses to let us justify ourselves against any propositional law, against any agreed and defined standard. The hope and expectancy of what can be, and this is limitless, make us what we are.

In the course of this book the authors indulge in a critique of contemporary attitudes which may strike many as extreme:

but once again it is this extremity, and the starkness of the contrast, evoked by a prophetic passion, which gives to this diagnosis its excitement and sense of desperate urgency. This is certainly an unsettling and disturbing book – and it is meant to be so. Essentially it is a book about an encounter with Jesus such as is involved in an effective committal to living. It is this same Jesus who has always given a uniqueness, a dynamic, and a revolutionary activism to Christian Faith whenever it has been faithful to its own loyalties. True, succeeding ages have clothed Jesus in the garb of their own time, and seen him as ministering to their own needs. The eighteenth century, against the background of a formal classicism, saw him as a rational Christ, and in making him relevant to their particular situation they ended by imprisoning him in a strait-jacket. The romantics broke free from this, and Jesus became to them, as to Schleirmacher for example, a Jesus of feeling. To the nineteenth century, in the full flood of Victorian optimism, a liberal Christ was preached and proclaimed, a Jesus who is the herald of progress, and the inaugurator of a new age. Against the shattering events of the twentieth century, with its devastating world conflicts, it is the crisis or eschatological Christ of Schweitzer and his successors who challenges men – men who like him live at the end of an age, and in a time of judgement.

Werner and Lotte Pelz present us with an existential Jesus, self-authenticating since his words become true as men live them out. Metaphysical problems may be insoluble and without meaning; the epistemological enquiry a cul-de-sac, a mere dead end; but this Jesus gives life abundantly when his words are taken for what they are, proclamations of existential truth and not propositional statements around which a coherent system of thought can be constructed.

Doubtless Jesus is bigger than all these attempts, conscious or unconscious, to contain him, though this does not mean that they are all of equal insight. I find Werner and Lotte Pelz's profession of faith significant, provocatively demanding, and uniformly disturbing. It is the latter because systems and traditional interpretations are so attractive in their security and tidiness; and the professional religious (such as myself) is often a slave to them. There are criticisms, of course, which I would wish to make, for I must regard the search for meaning and the desire to find an ontology as themselves existential, in the sense that they arise within experience itself. But *God Is No More* is an impressionistic work of art. Its coherence is not that given by formal design, but will be found in experience by the man who commits himself to the words of Jesus. Its force flows from the rich particularity of the response to living which it enshrines.

I hope many will read this book, and in a mood of receptivity, I am myself grateful to have been challenged by a work of this kind, which gives priority to Jesus in this way.

EDWARD CARPENTER

Little Cloister, Westminster Abbey,
10 *October* 1962.

CHAPTER ONE

Clarifications

CRITIQUE AND OPPORTUNITY

OURS is an age of perplexity. We suffer acutely from an *embarras de richesse*. We never had the choice of so many ideologies, philosophies, *Weltanschauungen*, religions and theologies, or were offered so many avenues of escape from the necessity of thinking about the 'meaning' of life, of our lived life. Surrounded by too many voices, we have lost our bearings. We have drifted into a way of life from which the questions that matter are largely excluded. We are preoccupied with what can be measured, manipulated, solved and discarded and about which brains' trusts cannot disagree – except for the moments of relaxation when we are willing to be entertained by their disagreements. We are at home among machines, gadgets, statistics and salary sheets, printed glamour and vicarious sex life. We are ill at ease among the actual problems of birth and death, love and friendship. We are disturbed by the untidiness of living. (Of course, there are always the seven thousand that have not bent their knee to Baal.)

It is true that the scientific revolution has brought much clarification where it was most desirable, that it continues to question our religious pretensions, that it destroys many old prejudices – even if at the price of creating a few new ones – that it is creating the conditions of a fuller life for the many who before had only been remembered in prayers and sermons. But I cannot agree that ours is the time of 'man's coming of age'. Our pre-occupation with *things*, with what is manageable; our reliance on *things*, whether machines, cars, television sets or hydrogen bombs; our belief that the way of least resistance, of efficiency, of time and labour saving is the way of wisdom; and that to be secure is to be alive: all this seems to be anything but mature. Our beliefs and pre-occupations appear to be a mixture of adolescence and senility, expressed in the confused aspirations and tired purposelessness of our time.

At such a time, when the centre of life has been evacuated for its suburbs and the fathers' furniture moved into the spare room, we become free – for better, for worse – for a new beginning. No longer claimed by any one of the many traditions that chatter round about us and want to lure us into apathy or fanaticism, we could once again listen attentively and without prejudice to the words of and about the man Jesus of Nazareth. We are no longer tempted to fit those words into a system – there are no systems left, except in the spare room. We need not try to fit them into the religious thought forms of our age – there is little religion left, except in the suburbs. Today we could be met by the simple, 'naked', 'untheologized' words of Jesus, and if we are lucky they will disturb, frighten, shock and puzzle us – as life itself.

The words of Jesus disturb me by their incredible promise, puzzle me by their impracticable demands, and frighten me by the unreasonable hopes they raise. Yet their promise and demands touch my fundamental desires so accurately that I am compelled to share my understanding of them, if for no better reason than to find out whether others will feel touched in the same way. In this book I want to convey my understanding and experience of my undogmatic, unecclesiastical, unsystematic encounter with the words of Jesus, and hope to show how they lay bare our ultimate desires, shock us in our ultimate complacencies and awaken our ultimate hope.*

THE WORDS OF JESUS

Throughout the book I shall use the phrase 'words of Jesus' to mean something simple though not unambiguous. It

* Attempts at evaluating human behaviour in the light of the words of Jesus should never degenerate into an academic discipline. Jesus does not generalize, does not tell *me* how *others* ought to behave. His words – if they find me – tell me what I could be and still fail to be. They make me see myself in a new light, eager to help others to look at themselves in that new, hopeful light.

denotes the words of men concerning the man Jesus which have come down to us in the book called the New Testament. I shall be thinking primarily, if not exclusively, of the Gospels when I use the phrase.

Now the words concerning Jesus consist of words about him and of words alleged to have been spoken by him. It is not easy to draw the line between these two kinds of words – to say whether a miracle story which is *about* Jesus is not simply a naïve concretion of a parable told *by* Jesus – and I shall make no effort to draw it. Nor do I claim to know how many of the words put into the mouth of Jesus – even in the Synoptic Gospels – were actually his very own. But, unlike the Form Critics, I am convinced that much, perhaps most, of Jesus' teaching was his own. This is a poetic conviction, an intuition, which carries no authority beyond its own persuasiveness – and is in this respect similar to the words which have established it. The alleged sayings of Jesus are, to my understanding, so full of pathos, irony, humour and a unique, sympathetic passion, that the supposition they could have been produced by the scattered communities of the early church seems to me absurd. I do not want to deny that pious and awkward hands have from the beginning interfered with those sayings and have sometimes succeeded in twisting them almost beyond recognition. But I believe that in most instances the imaginative ear can still pick out the sound of an intensely personal, hopeful and human voice. This book will have to show whether my conviction is convincing. (May I add that the problem of authenticity is ultimately not a scholar's problem, since it is not a question of authorship but of relevance – just as the ultimate justification of the Iliad does not lie in its Homeric parentage but in its beauty.)

When I read the New Testament I am met by the words of Jesus. I purposely do not say the 'Word of God', the 'Word of Christ'. (If the New Testament writers often employ such terms, it is because for them *God* and *Christ* – just as sacrifice, salvation, etc. – were existential terms. For us they are not.) The authority of the words of Jesus – if any – resides in themselves. Unless they convince and convict me, nothing in heaven or earth can compel me to accept them, or convince me of their truth or usefulness – certainly not a belief that Jesus was 'God' or the 'Son of God'. This is their freedom and their power: where they have been heard as they want to be heard, they awaken a desire and a hope which find their expression in the belief that he who speaks them '*lives*'. But: *I do not believe in the truth of the words of Jesus because I believe that he lives. I believe he lives when I am persuaded to believe in the truth of his words.**

We should therefore try hard not to let these words become part and parcel of our moral, philosophical or religious landscape – just as we would not treat the words of a friend in that fashion. We never quite succeed, as this would challenge our securities. The attempt to disentangle them from our system-weavings, to let them face us, is all the more urgent. We should not try too hard to smooth out apparent contradictions or to establish an overall harmony. The words of Jesus should come to us with the freshness of a unique observation made by *another* in a conversation taking place now, always now. When they strike us by their unexpectedness and newness, we have been successful – at least for the time being – in our efforts to listen.

What does it mean to listen? I truly listen, not when I – as so often – receive and understand the words of another according to the interpretation I had given to them in a former 'meeting'; but when I meet them as entirely new and fresh, as surprising, because they are telling me something which – in fact – I have not heard before, either because the speaker is new, or because he has something new to tell me, or because I myself am not the same person I was when I last heard those words.

The words of Jesus are always 'before us', never grasped, understood, fulfilled; always *to be* grasped, *to be* understood, *to be* fulfilled. Jesus did not leave a complete and coherent system

---

*All reports concerning Jesus' teaching come to us in an indirect and often ambiguous manner. Their historical and textual ambiguity stresses their 'innate' authority, just as the general uncertainty as to their contexts warns us against giving them too local a habitation and a name.

of teaching, presumably because he did not want to impose an external pattern on the gloriously diverse patterns of this world and our human relationships. His words open vistas into the possibilities of this world. He did not come to give answers. Life is not primarily a puzzle or a problem. It is primarily life, and Jesus told us how it can be lived. The words do not lay down laws. The 'law kills', and only the spirit by which a man lives makes him alive.[1] Jesus addresses people that 'do not know the law'.[2] The Pharisees understood that better than many modern – Pharisees.*

The words of Jesus urge us to interpret life in the light of the hope they raise in us. Such interpretation will never be more than an exploration, a quest, a probing of possibilities. It cannot be the expression of what we *know*. It can only be a pointing towards something – a listening to something – we *hope* to be true.

It is our dilemma that we do not *know* how to live. When we think we do, we are already half dead. At our best we have the courage to experiment, explore, risk. The words of Jesus assure us in our quest, they make us understand our human condition as a quest, as a beginning. When we seek, so they promise, we shall find. When we ask, we shall be answered and when we knock it will be opened to us. On the other hand, they insist that we have ceased to be human – have become inhuman, subhuman, 'gods' – when we think we *have* found, *have* been answered.[3] (All truly human thought and action gives expression to the belief that we are not 'gods', that everything we do can never be more than a searching, questioning, knocking.[4])

* The words of Jesus do not point to a 'truth'. They are 'truth'. They are not *means* to be discarded when the *end* has been reached. They are our 'end' – as a friend is an 'end' in himself. In as far as Jesus lived his words, was true to his words, we can say he is the sum of his words, that he is 'the Word' and that today he lives in his words, comes to life for us in and through his words.

THE WORDS OF LIFE

Every action of ours expresses the faith and hope by which we live. If such faith and hope be insignificant, our actions are bound to remain so, however world-shaking their repercussions may be. If our faith and hope are significant, our actions will be so, however private and intimate their consequences may remain. An action is significant – signifies something beyond itself – when it tries to fit meaningfully and purposefully into a larger pattern; when, though an end in itself, it needs a wider context in which to find a further fulfilment; when it needs someone or something from beyond itself in order to be completed.[5]

We cannot help feeling that our actions are fated to final futility, final insignificance; that all human striving is cannibalistic: it feeds on its own kind and ends by swallowing itself. And yet it expresses my strongest desire, namely to keep alive, to give to myself and keep for myself what I can neither give nor keep: life, growth, joy, love. Striving is also made futile by the fact that my neighbour's ambition feeds on my failure and mine feeds on his; by the fact of death which conditions us from the moment we realize our mortality.*

In the words and acts of Jesus we are faced by someone whose striving was not directed towards keeping alive, but simply towards living. ('If you want to keep your life, you will lose it.'[6]) He did not betray his life for the sake of keeping it. He did not refuse to 'live' his life for fear of losing it. And therefore his words *live*; he *lives* in his words and fascinates us.

We respond to his words when we begin to live as people who hope that they shall live, who believe quite simply that life is worth living, that death does not devalue it.[7]

It is characteristic of Jesus' life that it was only a beginning.

---

* The death wish is our unconscious reaction to the apprehension of our futility. We want to be irresponsible, escape from the false responsibility imposed on us by our ambitions whose end – finis as well as telos – is death. The hydrogen bomb is an illustration of the ambivalence of our ambitions: there is nothing more powerful to protect what we have, there is nothing more self-defeating.

It needed others to complete it. [8] It could be fulfilled only after his death. It *needed* death for its fulfilment. It was a stretching forward into the future even in face of death. The life of Jesus was the *incarnation* of the hope that for the true business of living death is irrelevant. [9]

To the unavoidable human question: what must we do in order to live? there is no human answer – and the words of Jesus never attempt to supply one. 'Leave all you have and all you are and follow me!' they say and thereby insinuate that we are not so much in need of an answer but of an answerer. It is part of the untidiness of life that it does not want to be solved but lived and to have someone to live with. Our lives could become the expression of our hope that men are worth while living with.

The words of Jesus begin to challenge us when we realize that what they promise is most desirable; when we feel disturbed by their intimation of a joy and fulfilment compared to which we feel frustrated, crippled, blind, deaf and dumb; when we suspect they may be *realistic* and our so-called realism no more than a refusal to live our lives.

LIGHT

It is not simply a metaphor or a simile, when Jesus is called the light of the world. In the biblical perspective – as well as in human life – the physical light is primary, the mental or moral 'light' is derivative, is a reflection of what first of all simply is. The light of the eye precedes and kindles the light of the heart and mind. We must see, before we can understand, and there must be something to be seen and something in the power of which it can be seen. Without light there is no growth, no discrimination, no order, no work, no play, no love. (Even love, although it can be consummated in darkness, can be conceived only in light.) Without light there is no human life. Even the blind can live as they do, only because there are others who can see.

Day by day, the returning light recreates the world, picking it up where it left it yesterday, picking out the loveliness and the scars, the beauty and the wrinkles, the daffodils and the weeds, the comfortable suburb and the slum, the cornfields and the battlefields. The light restores the memory and reveals its limitations; it clarifies, defines and elaborates. It can be merciful and merciless, according to the situation it reveals, according to our readiness for it. It adds a new dimension to our life. It enriches and complicates it. It liberates and betrays us. We can walk freely in the light, we can dance, we can find our way – we are discovered. And what we can find in darkness is only in memory of the light. Light gives us purpose and for every purpose we need light – whether to study or to crack a safe.

Light is indefinable. Even the scientists seem to find it difficult to catch it in a satisfactory formula. It has no shape or colour, yet gives shape and colour to all things. It has no local habitation, yet gives 'place' to everything. It is swift as thought and cannot be overtaken. It is still like the statue around which it lingers. It yields to all and clarifies, defines, judges and forgives in the yielding. All our efforts have to be exposed to it, and its evaluation has to be accepted by the sane. Light can sometimes be turned off, it can never be contradicted. Its victory is effortless, its impartiality is uncompromising, its promise is unshakable – 'as long as the sun and the moon and the stars last', it will not fail.

Light cannot be possessed, preserved, stored. It can only be used, accepted, acknowledged. One cannot boast of having it, using it, having seen it, having seen by it. One can only be grateful for it, rejoice in it, work by it. At times, one can direct it: into this corner, on to that screen, that page, that face, towards an invading plane or an escaping bird. There are times, when one simply has to let oneself be directed by it.

In this sense, the words of Jesus are the light by which we live. They return upon us with the repetitiveness of the recurring day. Over and again they retrieve the chaotic human landscape; recreating a certain order simply by illuminating it, forcing us to see it as it *is*, to see ourselves as we are. Their probing clarifies, defines our situation. It vastly complicates our black-white simplifications of the darkness. It is mercifully merciless in the obliteration of all illusions – whether feared or loved. His words 'discover' us, betray our whereabouts. They enable us to see our way and to recognize that we are not on the way yet. They uncover us and, in as far as we are not overcome by our nakedness, they liberate us. They introduce a new dimension into our life.

Like light, the words of Jesus are homeless, patternless, express no system, belong to no *Weltanschauung;* yet they 'put in their place' everything they meet. They are indefinable and yet define clearly what is most hidden. They do not compel, they do not impose themselves on us. They yield like light and judge us in the yielding.[10] Like light, the words of Jesus cannot be contradicted. But we can turn our back on them or draw the blinds. They cannot be 'kept'.* But we have always the chance to turn and face them. Unlike doctrine or dogma, they do not simplify. On the contrary, they open our eyes to the infinite complexity of life.

LOADED WORDS

Modern man is right to be suspicious of big, dogmatic assertions and of 'loaded' words. We often employ words which, by reason of their historical or liturgical solemnity, are an evasion rather than an expression of thought. We are tempted to use terms which, to some of us, seem persuasive, because of their powerful and evocative associations. We forget that to the many who do not share our memories the words sound hollow. Many of our arguments are really incantations. They re-convince us, because we are convinced already or answer questions which are leading questions. They impose a semblance of reasonableness and coherence on our experience, because we have grown up in a milieu where such coherence was implicitly taken for granted. Our arguments are useless when directed towards the man outside our esoteric circle, since he is by definition the one who is not convinced yet. He, too, may ask leading questions, but certainly not such as will lead to our answers. Perhaps he has had the misfortune of not

*In the sense of both: to hold, preserve and: to obey, fulfil.

having been taught how to neglect or ignore that kind of evidence in his experience which makes it difficult to recognize a coherence and reasonableness in it.

If we want to address that man to make him conscious of what the 'light' has revealed to us – and the proof of any revelation is in the desire to reveal it – we have to make a ruthless attempt to discover what we really believe, what is actually in our minds and hearts – though we may be shocked by what we find there. We have become slaves of our loaded words, because we are afraid of facing the 'truth' that is in us and which alone we can convey convincingly.[11]

The words of Jesus are far removed from any jargon or specialized terminology – though they, too, of course, are time-conditioned. That is why they have retained a surprising freshness underneath the exceeding great weight of glory we have heaped upon them in the course of the ages. They are as simple and ambiguous, as direct and baffling, as apparently contradictory as ever. (At times, when we do not want to hear them, but only want to explain them, they are as incomprehensible as ever.)

THE MIRACLE OF LIFE

Any truly human encounter creates an unprecedented situation and awakens hopes and expectations. An encounter with the words of Jesus – when they move us and involve us – awakens incredible expectations: They tempt us with what our hearts most desire, face us with a possibility that is not ours and promise – almost lightly – to give us what our efforts cannot hope to achieve. 'Do this,' they say, 'and you shall live.' Or rather: 'Because you shall live, do this'.[12]

At the heart of the oldest tradition we find the belief that the words of Jesus promise life and have the power to give it, that the promise may be believed, because the power has been demonstrated. The miracle stories seem to have been even more important to the *first* followers of Jesus than his teaching. In all the Gospels the miracle precedes the teaching and preaching. Whether or not we reject any or all of the miracle stories as products of an untutored imagination or unscientific observation, whether or not the 'miraculous' is still meaning-ful to us, still able to communicate an experience, the fact remains that the words of Jesus were experienced, from the beginning, as a promise of something that can only be des-cribed as health, wholeness, fulness, abundance of life, 'salva-tion' – which are experienced by the healthy, the abundant, by those full of life, as the most miraculous things in life. This fact still best explains why Western man has not been able to disentangle himself altogether from their persuasiveness and challenge.

What the words of Jesus promise us is, in the strict sense of the word, incredible. We can *not* believe it. On the other hand, they promise what, above all else, we would like to believe. 'He that believes in me shall live, though he die'.[13] They promise a relationship that cannot be broken and claim that *we* shall not be broken, when we accept this relationship. They promise that there will be a beginning beyond our end, a ful-filment beyond our failures, a meaning beyond the decay of our purposes, life beyond the life we can guard, keep, protect, defend and prolong.

The words of Jesus make us realize that we cannot, just can *not* believe in the possibility of what we most desire.[14]

ILLUSION OR PROMISE

The words of Jesus drive us to the point where we are threatened with the discovery that our ultimate desire is our ultimate illusion – unless we make the words of Jesus our ultimate desire; which we cannot do until they have persuaded us. We cannot help living by one illusion or another, whether it be an illusion of faith or of unbelief. Yet we fail to realize that this is our predicament, until the words of Jesus have put themselves into the place of our illusion. Even then they will lose none of their ambiguity, and if we believe we can make them unambiguous and assured, we have misunderstood them.[15]

There is no possibility for man to find the 'truth' that is assured and will assure him – though this is precisely what we have always wanted to find. Life, by its very nature, is insecure – so is love, joy, hope – and whoever wants to accept life fully, must accept its insecurity. Not to do this means to fall into an even greater illusion, namely that of believing that we can dispel illusions, go beyond ourselves, beyond life, that we can judge, 'become gods'. (The desire for certainty is a peculiar aspect of the death wish.)

I do not want to maintain that every illusion is *only* an illusion or equally illusory. I simply want to stress that it is not possible for us ever to say more than I believe this to be true for me, I hope it is true, I wish it were true. The question we have to ask is therefore not whether something is or is not an illusion, but by which illusion – let us by all means call it truth – we would best love to live. Are we most strongly tempted by the illusion of disillusion, or by the illusive fulfilment our society holds before us by means of its hidden persuaders, or by a revolutionary illusion? Or – realizing that we cannot escape from the necessity of making one illusion or another the measuring rod of our life – would we like to let ourselves be tempted by the promise implicit in the words of Jesus? Would we like to follow him rather than anyone or anything else – knowing that we cannot help following someone or something?

But who is Jesus that we should follow him? There are no satisfactory answers, just as there are none to the questions of a young woman as to why she should accept *this* young man. As a matter of fact, as long as we still ask we had better not follow,[16] because we cannot. As with all other illusions, as with friends and lovers, we can accept the promise of Jesus only when we cannot help accepting it.

Only this much we might perhaps add: Jesus' promise and demands are summed up in the words 'follow me' – whatever that may mean. This is to say that our response, whether it be yes or no is a decision and a committal. No other man has insisted like Jesus on the absoluteness of decision. None has dared, as he dared, to tie up our decision with his person.

FREEDOM AND HOPE

When a blind man receives his sight, a completely new dimension is added to his life. He is given a new freedom of movement, a new independence of decision, a new sphere of appreciation. His life is enriched beyond any possible expectation. When a deaf man is made to hear, a new world of understanding, friendship and beauty is opened to him, a new resonance is given to his whole experience. What he can now hear will not all be good and enlightening, but the fact that he can hear it will always be good and can always lead to enlightenment. A dumb man who regains his speech will discover that in becoming articulate towards others he becomes more articulate within himself. He will mature through his new possibility of expression. He will also be tempted to say many unnecessary things and leave unsaid what now he should say. For the chronically sick who is cured, there will not only be the great rejoicing in the flexing of his muscles, there will also be new burdens to be taken up. He will now have to carry what till then carried him. Together with the weariness of sickness he will leave behind its irresponsibility. The leper, cleansed and restored to the community, will have to start work, but will also be free once more to embrace his wife and children and to shake the hands of his friends. He becomes free to commit himself – and that is his freedom.

In the words of Jesus we meet the promise of wholeness. They promise to add a new dimension to our experience, a new maturity to our hearts and minds, a new lightness to our actions and decisions. They promise a new freedom within a new commitment: 'This do, and you shall live.' We test the promise by letting our life express the hope that it will be kept. And this we cannot do unless we really desire what is promised.

Our question therefore should be: What must we do in order so to learn the business of living – of seeing, hearing, talking, laughing, – that we shall long for more life? How can we learn to let ourselves be so 'frightened' by the promise of life that we shall crave for what life alone can fulfil? How can we learn to live now, as if there were only life before us? How dare we let ourselves be directed by what we most desire? How dare we live in the incredible hope that we shall get it?

CHAPTER TWO

Justification

WESTERN man has been – and still is – haunted by the words of Jesus. Even today he finds it difficult to escape from the insinuations of their promise, from the illusive hopes they raise. These words compel us to adopt certain attitudes and still make certain responses unavoidable. Implicitly and explicitly, before our private conscience and before an election meeting, in calling a nation to arms and a man to a more honest assessment of his motives, we feel the urge to justify our actions and motives in the light of those words. The modern agnostic, atheist, or European communist demonstrates – often more clearly than the religious man – how difficult it is to extricate oneself from their subversive influence.* Western man is not 'christian' – certainly not 'more christian' than the 'east' – but the words of Jesus have conditioned our attitude and given a peculiar flavour to our hypocrisies as well as to our sincerities.

Our longstanding eagerness to justify ourselves before those words, has placed us in a most ironic situation – Kierkegaard called it 'christendom'. We feel compelled to justify ourselves before – and in the light of – the words of Jesus, though they are at pains to persuade us that our life is not justified, as long as we feel the need to justify it. Jesus tempts us, we said, by means of our deepest longing: 'because you shall live, do this.' Now if we love doing what we are doing or at least are trying to do what, in the given circumstances comes nearest to what we should love doing, we shall feel no need to justify ourselves. If, on the other hand, we do what we do not love doing, what does not take us towards that which we most profoundly long for, if our desires are split and we realize that we are failures, we should, one would think, *not* want to justify

*Nietzsche, the most cogent and devastating critic of that influence, is the most striking example of a modern Jacob.

ourselves, for a justified failure means despair.* The words of Jesus, though making us feel our failure most poignantly by confronting us with our pristine ambition, urge us not to find reasons for it, not to settle down as failures. They try to persuade us that no failure is irreparable, that there is always hope. But hope, as we all know, is often painful and distressing – much more so than any 'carrion comfort'.[1] And that is why the words of Jesus instead of luring us back into our hope, often only tempt us to apologize for not letting ourselves be persuaded.

THREE ASPECTS OF JUSTIFICATION

As I am not using the word 'justification' in any technical connotation, but in its idiomatic, vague, existential usage, let me illustrate its meaning.

1. Justification by convention

A pattern of inherited beliefs, assumptions, prejudices, is the implicit justification of most of our actions and attitudes. This only partly conscious pattern is largely responsible for establishing that precious and dangerous equilibrium – desired by the psychiatrist, abhorred by the prophet – called a good conscience or, in moral philosophy, invincible ignorance. Our doings are the expression of our beliefs; our complacency is the sign that we take our beliefs for granted. For instance: how we bring up our children or want them to be brought up, the factors that determine our choice of a job for ourselves and for them, are the 'incarnation' of our belief that 'God helps those that help themselves' and that the 'devil takes the hindmost'. We deceive ourselves, our wife, our children, our public – and half-truths are deceptions – because we believe that 'peace' is more important than the 'truth' as we see it – 'and anyway, who are we to believe that our truth is important'. We concentrate on the cultivation of our back-garden,

---

*Much modern literature is fascinated by the inevitability of failure. It has justified failure, made us feel justified in being failures. It is therefore a literature of despair.

because we believe it is about as much order as we are allowed to establish in this world. We take out a life-insurance, but do not like to make ourselves 'friends by means of the mammon of unrighteousness'[2] – e.g. reduce substantially our own standard of living for the sake of those backward areas on whose development our life depends – because we believe that human prudence is wiser and more practical than the words of Jesus. The politician compromises as a matter of course, for it is taken for granted that success is more important – or, at least, more powerful, efficient, expedient – than the idea in the service of which one hopes to succeed. The citizen is satisfied with casting an occasional vote and is only too ready to turn a blind eye on the distortions and perversions of his own society – 'thank God that I am not like other men' – taking for granted that it is virtuous to keep himself to himself, not to 'interfere' in the lives of others, believing that privacy and private property are inviolable. Such are the kind of actions – there are many more – we can perform with a good conscience, because they are justified implicitly by the complex of ideas and feelings which are the result of our grandfathers' wisdom and prejudices. And these ideas and feelings in turn are justified by death, are the expression of the belief that 'tomorrow we are going to die'.

2. *Active Justification*

Secondly, there are the things we do to justify our belief, the action we perform to justify a personal conviction, a vision, a hope. The artist's work is an example of that kind of action. In face of incomprehension, derision, his own doubt and despair, he *must* give shape to what he has seen, in the hope that the shape he creates will justify the significance of his vision. The revolutionary, for better, for worse, is ready to make frightening decisions, because he is convinced that the order which will follow the chaos is going to justify the justice of his ideal. The businessman who takes a risky step must hope that the consequences will justify the risk.

Whenever we take a risk, laying ourselves open to the surprises of uncertainty, we let our works justify our faith. Such actions are far more exhilarating than those justified by our accepted beliefs. The health of a personal life, the health of a society, can best be gauged by man's capacity for such action. Where the incentive and the possibilities for it wither away, life decays. All human 'progress' is the fruit of such activity. And yet, it is as full of ambiguity as progress itself. Not only can creative action lead to 'evil' as well as to 'good', but it is bound to become in the long run just another part of that pattern which is the inheritance as well as the burden of future generations and the corruption of their springs of action. (For example, the teaching of Jesus is turned into a religion. The Bible as well as the plays of Shakespeare or Sophocles become fields for scholarly research and counter-research.)

3. *Delegated Justification*

Thirdly there are the actions – responses to the various demands of social and personal relationships – that are justified by somebody else's belief, whether that belief be of the active or passive kind. These acts of delegated justification include the non-committal execution of an order, the 'irresponsible' obedience demanded in impersonal institutions such as industry or the army; the kind of cooperative response to a given policy as is demanded of the civil servant; the committed personal trust and identification of purpose as may exist between layman and expert, patient and doctor, apprentice and master, the disciple and his teacher. However, among men, and this is our solidarity, responsibility cannot be ultimately delegated. Upon closer scrutiny, any act of obedience will disclose itself as either one or the other kind of action described in (1) and (2). Where our obedience is automatic, it corresponds to the action that is justified by our accepted beliefs. Where our obedience coincides with our hopes and desires, it will correspond to those creative actions which try to justify the belief they express.

THE CRITIQUE OF THE WORDS OF JESUS

The words of Jesus do not necessarily abolish all assumptions that justify our behaviour. They expose them all to a radical criticism by bringing them into the light of consciousness. I can no longer feel sure of being justified when I exert myself in the hope that my child will 'get on'. Where once dark, tribal promptings paraded as moral wisdom, stands now an intimation of an altogether different kind of consummation.[3] I can no longer take it for granted that I am justified in cultivating my back garden virtues. In place of my former prudent apathy, I now find words that tease me into believing that I have something worth teaching to all nations,[4] even to the ends of the world. As a politician I am not necessarily justified in making the necessary compromise. Instead of the persuasive whisper of my primeval desire for victory at any price – disguised as the wisdom of ends and means – I am troubled by the echo of a most paradoxical victory.[5]

The works which are meant to justify our belief and vision are also criticized by the words of Jesus. The artist can hear the warning against complacency, against escape into a private world, against prostitution of his gifts and, above all, the call to remain true to his nature.[6] The revolutionary is reminded of the ambiguity of an achievement based on violence,[7] the businessman of the ultimate irrelevance of his most relevant investments,[8] the planner of the peripheral nature of everything than can be planned,[9] and the conservative of the folly of wanting to keep what he has.[10]

All delegated responsibility is made problematical by the words 'follow me', which call us *into* responsibility and responsiveness and remind us that a relationship which diminishes our responsibility is not desirable.[11]

The words of Jesus reveal the true nature of justification which is not the vindication of the justice and 'rightness' of what we are or have achieved, but the revelation of what we could become. They hold before us the challenge of a possibility that could become our life. In reaching out towards that possibility, so they promise, we shall be justified. Jesus himself believed in that possibility, and in as far as he continues to persuade us, his belief is justified – he is alive, and his 'aliveness' fascinates us.

Jesus thought of life as something absolute, indestructible. (Terms like 'resurrection', 'eternal life', 'salvation' try to communicate the incommunicable, or rather, clothe it in words that had strong, parabolic significance at the time.) For him all life is a parable of life as it could be and will be, or better: as it is now if we understand it as a parable.[12] He is so intensely preoccupied with the *meaning* that for its sake he is willing to die, although he loves life. And his words still persuade us that the life he sought and lived is meaningful, that is, indestructible. They have certainly persuaded Western man – unlike the men who have fallen under the spell of other guides – to search for a meaning and purpose in life. For better, for worse, we are pursued by the double question: '*What* do I live for?' and 'What do *I* live for?'

Here again the situation is full of irony. Our search for meaning – stimulated by the words of Jesus – has deteriorated into a search for security. (Heaven and Hell, infallibility of persons or institutions, 'Confessions' and denominations, ideologies and insurance companies are all expressions of our search.) We have surrounded the words themselves with so much religious and metaphysical glory, that we now feel absolutely safe in listening to them. Yet we have misunderstood something of crucial importance, if we fail to realize that the words cannot call us into true responsibility, unless they come to us – as to the original disciples – with no other authority save that of their inherent persuasiveness. They lure us into a life the truth of which we cannot discover except in the living; a life we cannot justify, because we can only hope that in living it we shall feel justified. They frighten us, because they seem to goad us into complete insecurity, all the more so, because they reveal the insecurity of our securities,[13] the meaninglessness of our meanings.[14] For that reason, we – just stirred enough to feel the need for some kind of response – try to justify our refusal to accept their offer of a meaningful life, i.e. to 'live in hope'. (And hope cannot be verified, since it is that which verifies us. For example, in marriage we are not meant to find out whether the 'ideal' of marriage is true for us, but whether we can become true to our ideal of marriage.)

ATTEMPTS AT JUSTIFICATION

1. Justified before our Neighbour

We are afraid of slander, of losing our reputation, losing face. As individuals, nation, party, church, we are eager to make an image of ourselves and to make it appear spotless in the sight of men. We spend much time and paper, as a nation much ammunition, on making the world appreciate what we are. We do and say many things to justify our life and achievement. We forget that when our achievements cease to justify themselves, no amount of 'explaining' will make others appreciate them. More important: we forget that what we are is not our achievement, but what the accidents of history have made of us. We are the provisional end-product of a process. We are the future of our past. If there is anything in us that is justified, our *future* will justify it. (Just as an apple tree – if it be one – is not justified by last year's harvest but only by that of next year and the year after.[15])

The words of Jesus – which are a part of the past that shaped us – make it clear that the desire to justify what we are is a perversion, since what we are is unjustifiable. Wars, famines and epidemics, crime waves, arms races, advertising and the entertainment industry, our own feelings of impotence in face of such disorders, should suffice to make us realize that what we are – and the state of affairs we have produced because we are what we are – is indefensible, that it would be very sad, indeed, if all this could be justified.

The words of Jesus urge us to look up, to look forward, not to believe it when people say: 'here, here'.[16] They tell us to feel satisfied when we are disturbed and to feel disturbed when we are complacent.[17] They ask us to dance for joy when people think that what we are doing is unjustified, for that is what they thought about their prophets, about the very people whom the future has justified.[18]

2. *Justified by Works*

We wish to be justified in what we do. This is a healthy desire if it means that we want our work to speak for itself – and for us in as far as it is a concrete expression of our nature. To wish for more – and we often do – is foolish.

(a) Our work cannot justify us. There is always much more to us than can be expressed in any work. Even the work of art cannot express the wholeness of its creator and the artist who thinks he is justified by his work, who fails to go beyond it, is not an artist.[19]

(b) When we do any work from ulterior motives instead of for its own sake, we have lost the organic contact and it profits us nothing.[20] (The fact that our society imposes much work on us which few men can love for its own sake, does not invalidate my statement. Much modern work is unprofitable.) The desire to be justified, appreciated, drives us into many labours we do not love, for the sake of a reward not inherent in the work. We want to advance, get more money, greater power. We shall get our reward and it will prove to us that our efforts were not justified.[21]

(c) Work not done for its own sake becomes corrupt and corrupting. It makes us avid of glory and bitter when we do not get it, censorious – pharisaical – because it frustrates our actual desires. It makes us want to die and hope for a Heaven where roles will be reversed. It shrinks our hopes – and therefore our capacities – for a man who wants to be justified by his work is not likely to attempt the impossible – which alone could justify him.[22] His work, in turn, will corrupt others by its pervasive insincerity, its 'deathliness'.[23]

(d) The wish for justification is the wish for the measurable, the possible. I want to get as many of my children as possible through the examination; I want so many more votes, so many more people in my shop, my cinema, my church. To achieve the measurable, I have to concentrate on the techniques which promise success. Yet success does not justify – it can easily stultify – and although we know it we continue to hunger for it.[24]

Life is justified by the imponderable, the unexpected, the impossible. It is justified – if at all – in the living, and in our work only when it is part of our living and when we are not anxious as to what men will say about us.[25]

3. Justified before our Conscience

We not only desire, but are encouraged, to consider our conscience as the final court of appeal. It is true that we can rarely do better than act in accordance with its dictates. Yet the fact that our actions do not aspire to anything nobler than the reaching of that state of complacency we call a 'good conscience' should make us feel uneasy. It is frustrating not to be able to do better than obey my conscience, i.e. the arbitrary experiences and prejudices of my group and my forebears. To justify myself before my conscience means to justify myself before the demands which any society in search of security makes on its members. (It might help to recall that the persecutors of the prophets have, on the whole, a good conscience.)

We are tempted to overestimate the significance of conscience, on account of its apparently universal presence. Every man, we are told, has at least a rudimentary knowledge of good and evil, right and wrong – though the contents of those terms vary according to time and place. There is no one, we are told, who is not at times encumbered or upheld by an inner resistance or insistence, by a voice saying: 'Do this!' and 'Do not do that!' Such statements seem to me of doubtful value. Modern study of anthropology and ethnology has reduced these generalizations to such vagueness that they have become meaningless. (The occurrence, in the heart of 'christian Europe', of such events as the Gestapo and SS mentality, the drift of a highly civilized nation into the openly condoned use of torture in a 'good cause', are further reminders of the almost infinite flexibility of human conscience.)

Yet let us grant that there is something irreducible behind that elusive term, a final insistence on decision, choice and discrimination. Even that or, perhaps, precisely that, can be explained most satisfactorily in psychological, sociological and historical terms. (A metaphysics of conscience is a luxury not a necessity.) Conscience is no more and no less than the ever renewed struggle on the part of the individual and that of society to arrive at some kind of 'correspondence', mutual adjustment, balance, peace. It is part of the cosmic tendency to find a common level, to come to rest, however many disturbances will have to be quelled and however many mountains levelled. Conscience – even an 'informed conscience' – is immanent. It is altogether 'of this world'[26] – and I see no reason to doubt that Caiaphas' decision to condemn Jesus as a blasphemer was a most 'conscientious' decision.[27]

For the words of Jesus disturb the conscience, undermine its security, prevent it from coming to rest. They tease and frighten us by revealing its inadequacy. They insinuate themselves into the place of conscience and reduce it to the role of the accuser, the persecutor – a part which in the Old Testament is assigned to the devil. The Sermon on the Mount and the parables of Jesus compel us to admire the logic which forces the conscience of the world to execute him who spoke them. Either the words of Jesus are made radically problematical by our conscience, or it is made radically problematical by them.

[I am convinced that christian *casuistry* is based on a complete misunderstanding: 1) Against all biblical evidence, casuistry takes conscience very seriously. Because it is the product of an established order desirous to perpetuate itself, casuistry does not understand that even on the pragmatic level there are times when the courage to act against one's conscience is required. (Of course, all authoritarian societies, whether churches, parties or nations, try to get a hold over the conscience of their members.)

2) Casuistry has never been able to shed those religious and metaphysical assumptions which are questioned most pertinently today and are no longer *assumed* by the vast majority of our fellow men.

3) Conscience is the sensitive nerve exposed to the 'dream', the possibility which did not seem to be ours. Casuistry has

often reduced itself ad absurdum by working towards a contradiction in terms: a 'good conscience'.

4) Casuistry has never been able to avoid explaining away the words of Jesus, for before those words we cannot have a 'good conscience' nor do we particularly want to have one. It has always been compelled to reduce them to principles, ideals, 'counsels' etc. It has been compelled by its own logic to integrate the words of Jesus into its own world picture, to make them immanent, undisturbing.

5) Casuistry is based on the psychological mistake of believing that man really and above all else wants peace, a 'good conscience'. It has fallen into the trap of taking our desires at their face value. But such volcanic eruptions as fascism demonstrate that the heart of man wants more than peace; that peace, balance, the equilibrium, does not liberate us. 'Our hearts are restless until they find rest in Thee.' and to such rest there is no casuistic short-cut. We are not free when we feel 'good'. We become free, when we are so radically challenged by something from beyond our achievements that we cannot help responding, 'repenting', turning, *moving and being moved*.

4. *Justified before 'God'*

Pharisaism is the subtlest form of idolatry. In place of conscience – not necessarily in contradiction to it – pharisaism posits the complex, externalized symbol of 'tradition', an amalgam of national and religious aspirations, of dark longings and mystical apprehensions, of metaphysical speculations and fragmentary experiences. The pharisaical god is a deification of the past, a glorification of the human achievement, a sheet anchor of the status quo. He is par excellence, a god that *has* revealed himself, *has* acted, *has* spoken, and who can therefore be understood, interpreted, who can be *seen* at work in history, who can be obeyed. He is an objectified god, an 'unperson', who can become the object of my decision, before whom I am free to say 'yes' or 'no', before whom I have justified myself as soon as I have said 'yes'.

Pharisaism substitutes the past for the future, the dead saint for the living sinner, the code for the challenge. I am a pharisee whenever I feel I *know*; when I think I *have* understood, when I am convinced I am right; when I say 'you must' rather than 'you may'; when I separate the commandment from the promise, the action from the reward or fulfilment; when I feel I *have* received what can only be asked and hoped for.[28]

The pharisee is not satisfied with his own conscience. He has the healthy desire for something bigger to worship, something which, at times, can override even his conscience, something before which he can bow in company with many of his peers. He wants an idol, an ideal, an ideology, something that justifies his desire to justify himself before it. He will usually find it convenient to bestow upon that something the name of whatever god there happens to be. Once upon a time that name was Yahweh and it was in that name that Jesus was crucified. Later on the name was Jesus and in that name the heretics were burned, the various pharisaical wars are blessed, the various 'unbelievers' are stigmatized. The pharisaical god is always 'our' god, 'my' god, who is called upon to defend 'our' way of life, our country, our heritage, our church, because it is taken for granted that, fundamentally, he has justified us in our ways: the pharisaical god is a useless god! For if we are justified already, a god would be a superfluity.

The pharisaical god bears a close resemblance to the Jungian archetype, the 'wise old man', the 'shadow'. He is the communal super-ego, the hypostasized 'archetype of meaning'. He epitomizes man's struggle to integrate the multitude of communal impressions and aspirations into a comprehensible whole where he can find a justified and justifiable place. As such he is performing a restraining and civilizing function. But he is not a 'he', but an 'it', an emanation of the social life, an 'epiphenomenon' of the economic process etc. It can give no further meaning to our life. When a man realizes this, he turns atheist or fundamentalist, communist or nihilist, 'Roman Catholic', 'Anglican' or 'Methodist'. He gives a new name to the shadow from which he cannot escape since it is his own.

(Pharisaism flourishes in the intellectual as in the 'moral' life. The conviction that I am right is as pharisaical as the belief that I am good. If pharisaism is an 'unjustifiable' attitude, then much of our philosophizing, theologizing and moralizing, is unjustifiable. Communal pharisaism is no better than the individual brand, only much more dangerous.)

The words of Jesus ask us to jump over our shadow or, more correctly, to forget it. 'Follow me,' they say – as Jesus once said to his disciples – and this implies no less than an invitation to forget all about gods and to concentrate our attention on our neighbour, from whom we are encouraged to expect much and who is asked to expect much from us. It also implies that if there be a God – and we have to admit that Jesus thought so – we can find him only in our neighbour, when our neighbour has become a friend. For only in a friend – not in a shadow, however exalted the name we give it – shall we meet the unexpected, the imponderable that astonishes and recreates us. Only before a friend we no longer want to justify ourselves, for he makes us want to do more than we *can* do – as the 'beloved disciple' knew. (John xiv, 12–17; xv, 12–17.)]

CHAPTER THREE

The Promise of Committal

EXPLORATION

EXPERIENCE always 'prevents' interpretation. This is our *dilemma*, because we find it hard to shed the conviction that we can learn from history, from experience, and often complicate today's problems by making the response that might have been adequate for the problems of yesterday – if we had made it yesterday. It is also our *salvation* – so I hope – as it will effectually frustrate the advent of those utopian nightmares in which man, having come to understand himself 'perfectly', will become perfectly conditioned.

No inquiry into the motives and motive powers of man's behaviour can therefore be more than an exploration. If we believe to know what we can only hope to rediscover in a lifetime of experimenting and think we have the answers – all moralism expresses such a conviction – we 'deceive ourselves'.[1]

Man is not liberated by pronouncements, rules and patterns; yet his persistent longing to have his 'I' absorbed in an overriding concern, will always make of the 'law'* his subtlest temptation. We long for the leader who does not ask for a response but gives answers, requires no committal but simply obedience, tells us what to do and relieves us of our responsibility. If we have no leader, we want a law, or constitution, or religion to perform his function. Tyranny in one form or another – whether of one or of many, of an ideal, idea or shared emotion or of brute matter – seems to be our unavoidable heritage, 'for we love to have it so'.[2] (The fleshpots of Egypt are most alluring when the alternative is the desert and manna. Perhaps we should not be too hard on the moral theologian when he is tempted to turn Jesus into a benevolent tyrant. It is human, all too human.)

*See Chapter 7.

Our hearts are made of recalcitrant and resilient material. They are easily impressed, they are hardly ever changed. They remain the same under the many changes of action, direction or motive. They stubbornly retain their limited ambitions, their death-bound hopes, their pathetic faith in their own beating. They are ready to clothe themselves into many ideologies, including christianity, in order to pursue their own devious ways more respectably. Yet the very smallness of their objectives is our greatest danger, for behind the conscious and definite desires of our hearts, dark and indefinable energies are at work that cannot always be contained but clamour for a creative – or destructive – outlet. Moral theology had made us aware of those dark forces long before the arrival of psychiatry, yet it rarely tried to grapple with them creatively and humbly. Moral theology, as well as the secular systems of morality which have grown out of it and away from it, has usually been satisfied with *damming up our archetypal impulses*, impressing our *unruly desires* into outward conformity, and using our '*infinite longings*' for the preservation of the status quo.*

OPPRESSIVE ORDER

Such methods of dealing with our dark energies have fatal consequences.

(1) The dammed up impulses will stagnate or find an unexpected outlet. Unless they are allowed to flow through the turbines, to become transformed into lifegiving energy, they will inundate the countryside. The monotonous recurrence of

---

*The moralist – philosopher or theologian – following in Plato's footsteps – without possessing Plato's boundless imagination – thinks it appropriate to impose upon life itself those checks and counterchecks by which an enlightened society protects itself against itself. He mistakes the necessary but superficial and unstable order of organized society for a metaphysical reality. He rarely questions the values of a given situation radically – he leaves that, unlike Plato, to the prophets. He is concerned with teaching men how to fit into the given civilization, how to accept, uphold and preserve it – often far beyond the time of its usefulness.

war, becoming more and more virulent throughout the civilized ages, is a reminder that we have not yet found the purpose to harness our 'dark energies'. In our own age, the glut of nuclear devices and nuclear policies is a warning that the time for finding such purposes may be short, that the task of looking for them has 'eschatological' urgency.

When the impulses stagnate, because they have been dammed up at the source as well as the mouth, they produce the weary and tired society of which we are members; apathy in face of joy as well as annihilation; futilities like the three-dimensional, technicolour, stereophonic television; a proliferation of methods without contents, of means without ends; an ever more rapid turning of wheels within wheels.

(2) When our *desires* are persuaded or compelled to conform to an external pattern – however high the standard, holy the motive, exalted the goal – we become hypocrites, pharisees, idolaters. Our very virtues will become something external, objective, dead. We become censorious, envious, jealous, ambitious, sanctimonious, pious, religious. Our real desire goes underground and burns the roots of sincerity, sensibility, sympathy and understanding, creating the desolate landscape of the industrial slum or modern subtopia, littered with Sunday newspapers, glamorized sex and the many other appurtenances of vicarious indulgence. Above all, the suppressed desire projects into the hearts of others its own frustrations, bitterness, and hatred: it creates the enemy.*

(3) Our 'infinite longings' are corrupted. By '*infinite longings*' I mean that complex of ideas, sentiments, intimations and partly understood insights, which persistently point towards a fulfilment beyond the gratification of the moment. We all have known them, at least in our childhood. They are the lure of the unknown – the positive complement to the Kierkegaardian concept of dread! – the condensation of all childlike expectations, the expression of our immaturity. They tease our adulthood with the promise of an impossible maturity. They

*See page 135 ff.

trouble us, for we fear they cannot keep what they seem to promise. They belittle our achievements in our own eyes.

Most of us are only too ready to accept the advice of the moralist and 'renounce the dream, renounce the vision'. But the boundless though elusive resources of those dream-makers cannot so easily be neglected or destroyed, though they may easily be diverted into serving an alien purpose. They can be changed from an intimation which challenges what we are by the hope of what we could be, into the assurance that we are already what we would be – that we have done our best. When this transmutation of our longings has taken place, we become fanatical or tolerant – ignorant of any other possibility – or simply respectable. The infinite possibilities that lay before us, now lie behind us, giving us that well known, wonderful feeling of security in our rightness. We become settled, complacent, immovable. We are ready to give our life in defence of 'what is', the status quo. All patriotism, nationalism, denomi-nationalism, all –isms – and also the easy tolerance that can put up with many of them at a time – are expressions of our mis-placed longings, examples of our 'idolatry' – and the most surprising are the christian churches.

We should have to accept the inevitable consequences of the repression of our vital energies, the prostitution of infinite longings – and the endeavours of the moralists would be at least partly justified – if there were no alternative. We should have to 'put up with life as it is', if the alternative meant the unbridled reign of our passions which, as we claim to know, leads into even graver servitude. Whether this is true, is at least doubtful. We now know that many of our 'wicked' desires are the result of inhibitions. It may well be that our passions, if permitted to grow in tenderness as well as in intensity, will turn out to be much more constructive than we dared hope. Altogether the alternative of 'law' or 'brute passions' is narrow and unreal and largely due to the un-fortunate influence of christian dogma and ethics.

More than any other tradition, christian dogma has per-suaded the 'western' mind to think in terms of abstract concepts and alternatives. It has – against all biblical warnings – imposed upon our thinking the categories of judgement, of either – or, of salvation – damnation, heaven – hell, election – rejection, good – evil, right – wrong, east – west. (Even our humanists and agnostics cannot help thinking in terms of those categories which makes many of their protests often sound very naïve.) Dogma has established this abstract order by transforming the biblical dialectic – the dynamic challenge of 'choose, today, between life and death', as worked out in Deuteronomy for example – into a cut and dried human alternative. (In this respect Marxism is a direct descendant of christian dogma.) But the biblical dialectic does not describe an ideological conflict between 'us' and 'them' – church and state, believer and unbeliever, left and right. It reveals an 'existential', intensely human struggle, fought out in a man's heart and on all levels of our social life, tearing the conscience, the church, the nation. It is the fight between our own beliefs and unbeliefs, hopes and despairs, our *dreams* and our desire to be *realistic*, between the challenge of love and the fear of loss, between the infinite possibilities of life and the strictly limited possibilities of death. This fight does not divide me from my neighbour but, primarily, from myself.

In the light of the words of Jesus I recognize that I am predominantly on the side which cannot help losing even if it should win: the side of resignation, disillusionment, the side without future. I also hear the promise that it need not be so, and accept it, by renouncing judgement rather than the 'vision'. Christian doctrine has rarely paid more than lipservice to the revelation of a possible human condition which is the Gospel. It has perpetuated a way of thinking which, though not responsible for all present ills, has made it easier for us to justify them.*

* The very fact that the church has a dogma which claims to be more than a tentative formulation, has encouraged us to put concepts in the place of living experience. No dogma can be more than a provisional formulation of a present apprehension, a question mark. As a matter of fact it has become much more: our pride, our security from doubt – even the doubt whether the other party or denomination may be right – it has

THE ALTERNATIVE

The words of Jesus – and this is what makes of them, if they be true, the Good News – try to persuade us that there is scope for our archetypal impulses, that there is a purpose that can order our unruly desires without cramping them, that our infinite longings point to our most intimate reality. They lure us into adventurous committal by means of a highly dangerous promise: 'Follow me ... and you shall see the heavens open'[3] – more than any lover has yet dared to promise. They call us into the reckless acceptance of ever shifting and changing human relationships, into unreserved committal to the explosive, a-moral, creative experience of love, friendship and companionship, into our adolescent dream of life, as into our true life. 'Sell all you have, give it away and come and follow me, if you want eternal life.'[4]

I am convinced that the original 'follow me' of Jesus is precisely such a call into reckless, unpremeditated friendship, for the sake of which a man is asked to leave father and mother and even his wife, if she be not the better friend. It is this call which makes Jesus unique among the great teachers. Unlike Buddha or Socrates he does not primarily offer wisdom, but simply himself. The great 'I am' passages of John's Gospel are the explications of the 'follow me': I, your friend, who lays down even his life for you, am your bread, your life, your light. But Jesus did not only demand committal. He committed himself without reserve to his friends, although he knew that they would betray him. He loved them to the end, and to be able to do that is, according to the words of Jesus, our hope.[5]

Now the disciples who first heard the call, were not called into a mystical relationship with a divine being, but into a very earthy and risky one with a homeless vagrant who promised

become our idol. It has for us the position the 'law' had for the Pharisees. When the methods of dogma – of an outworn, provincial metaphysics – are taken from the scholastic playing fields and applied to the business of living, the results are disastrous.

them that in their mutual love they would find all they had ever hoped for. In the same way, the words of Jesus do not try to entice us into a mystical relationship with himself, but into the acceptance of the kind of relationship which was epitomized by what happened between him and his disciples. In other words: they ask us to follow our neighbour as hopefully as Peter, John, and the others once followed him, and to become the sort of neighbour whom others can follow hopefully.[6]

Unfortunately there is only one relationship left to us modern men which can reflect something of the completeness of involvement demanded and promised by Jesus, namely marriage. It is a great pity that we know very little nowadays of the friendship Plato praises in his Dialogues and the old Chinese in their poems. (And what does it matter that such friendships were often based on a homosexual attraction?) It is a pity that we have not yet reached the maturity where marriage could make us ready for many and diverse loves which would not destroy but enhance our life together. It is the greatest pity that we no longer seem to have any experience of the fellowship which knits together a small community, as the disciples were knit together – or is our idea of that communion only a dream, on a level with that into which the words of Jesus call us today? I use marriage as an example of committal, not because I believe that it is the only one or the best, but because it is the one of which we still have some experience.

MARRIAGE

The Concrete Hope

Marriage involves us completely, body and mind, and therefore tests us, makes and unmakes us as men and women. It is gift and achievement – always both – and requires that complete and always changing responsiveness which alone keeps us human and alive. We are reminded day by day, that we 'realize' the joys it promises through our readiness to enter into the responsibilities it brings, that all joy grows out of responsiveness and responsibility, that irresponsible joy is paltry and joyless responsibility inhuman. It helps us to respond to the pathos and loveliness of the whole of mankind in this man and this woman. It makes us wonder whether there is any other way towards the love of mankind except through a friend or a wife.

When the church, through the doctrine of the indissolubility of marriage, wants to say to bridegroom and bride: 'This is your partner, *through* him – or her – you may discover the whole of mankind. If you want to by-pass him – or her – because you want more, you will discover that you get less,' it points towards a real insight. When it turns this insight into a law, it obliterates it and becomes responsible for distorting our understanding of marriage more gravely than any number of divorces.

To separate responsibility from joy, and duty from love, corrupts man's personality at its roots. It undermines his hope in life – and tempts him to substitute for it a hope in 'heaven' where things will be different. When we destroy the unity of desire and obligation we turn man into a schizophrenic, 'moral' animal.

Marriage is the incarnation of our hope. Our vague, adolescent longings, desires, ambitions and dreams are brought down to earth by a most concrete encounter at the moment when the other one is still altogether haloed by intimations of immortality. It is a resurrection experience. It puts our dreams to the test – or us. We soon learn either to judge our dreams in the light of our everyday experience of growing familiarity, or we continue to judge our everyday life in the light of our dream.

Most modern 'western' marriages have at least a promising beginning. The emotions called 'falling in love' may be illusory, but they are hopeful illusions, while our later wisdom is simply an unhopeful one. Once we expected an amazing consummation, and our marriage will find out how much truth there was in us when we expected so much: Will the fact that today's consummation rarely lives up to yesterday's hope make us cynical, resigned or reasonable? Or will

we continue to badger the future for the postponed fulfilment, refusing to take 'no' – even the wisest 'no' – for an
answer?

(This view of marriage is conditioned by the New Testament understanding of life as something that is always moving
towards more life. On the other hand, our understanding of
marriage may help us to solve one of the great riddles of the
New Testament tradition: the fading eschatological hope. Is it
really a question as to who expected what and when? Who was
right, Jesus or John, the early or the later Paul? Or are the dis-
crepancies – between those that expected the last day tomorrow and those that were not sure – simply the expression of a
tension which is the tension of life? – an intimation of the fact
that we cannot understand our hope for tomorrow except as
a recapture of the intensity of yesterday's hope? 'Unless you
become like little children, you will never enter the kingdom
of heaven.'[7] Paradoxically, this may explain why the words of
Jesus can only be understood by adults; why Abraham, the
archetype of hope, was called when he was old;[8] why the
prophets always harken back to the glorious intensity of the
desert courtship.[9]

But if it is true that a hope cannot become meaningful,
unless it refers back to the intensity of an experienced – even
if frustrated – hope, then the task of striving for and creating
the conditions which make that experience possible, is of
supreme importance. We must do everything in our power to
give substance to men's hopes, in order to protect them – and
ourselves – from the fanatical intensity of the 'destitute' whose
looking forward has no 'substance'.)

'Realization'

Marriage is an 'incarnation' of love. It is simply the expression, the open acknowledgement of a living affection that
binds two people together. Beyond that, love knows no rules,
since it cannot be brought into or kept in existence by anything but itself. We know this at the beginning of our relationship, when our turbulent instincts have only just condensed

their infinite longings into an embraceable figure, when our enthusiasm is not yet tempered by experience and there is still much innocence in us.

Unfortunately, 'incarnations' are fleeting and ambiguous. However overwhelming the 'realization' of 'love, it remains an intimation and a promise. Yet love lives in such 'realizations', in our efforts to recapture its original ardour – no matter on what level – in our eagerness to be nagged once more by its evasive promise. Of course, we all love love. But we also love peace, and love is restless; we love security, and love is always insecure. We thirst for the palpable fulfilment, and love – demonic and spiritual[10] – turns every fulfilment into a new thirst. This tension between the desire for the certainty of death and the half-frightened craving for the uncertainties of living, is reflected in our loving. We rather chain the beloved than live in the uncertain hope of always being able to charm her – or him. We rather tie her to us by laws and convention, than by the continually renewed effort to captivate her and to be captivated. We long for the love we can have without actually loving. To hide this paradoxical desire from ourselves – apart from talking about faithfulness, loyalty and morality – we pretend to a consummation and permit our desire for security to drive underground our desire for life. When we discover that the consummation cannot be forced, we become resentful or resigned, we begin to look for it elsewhere or cease expecting it altogether – and respectability can be more soul-destroying than adultery. (Mistaking the fireside chairs for the terminus, the photographs on the mantelpiece and in the album for our life, we are bound to mistake the undertaker for our future.)

Marriage gives us the opportunity to re-enact, in word and motion, in memory and expectation, the drama of our beginning. Every vital decision could reflect the adventure of courtship, every act should be the climax of another time of wooing, for love cannot be had at any other price than that of a new declaration of love which is not sure of the answer. Each marriage evolves its peculiar, almost liturgical repetitiveness which often degenerates into a spiritless observance leading to jealousy and possessiveness, as we are no longer sure of the value of what we possess. On the other hand, this liturgical rhythm can become the life-storing and life-giving memory of the body, as the always changing and unchanging erotic play gathers into itself memories which the mind cannot contain. It strengthens our hopes for tomorrow by keeping them in contact with our hopes of yesterday.

Spontaneity

Eternity, if at all imaginable, can be imagined only as spontaneity, as joy. (Everything else would be 'hell'.) Only joy, whether experienced or longed for, found or lost, is in need of and longs for eternity. Joy is spontaneous and commands our spontaneous obedience. (Like the words of Jesus, it is its own authority.) Only what we do *for the joy of it* is ultimately worth doing and well done, and wants to be done again. Our desire for 'repetition', for eternity, is the measure of our original joy. (Promiscuity is such a paltry thing, because it must be a paltry joy which from the beginning does not thirst for eternity.) Marriage gives us much time for 'repetition', and in this way tests and reveals our desires.

It also enables us to grow in spontaneity through its ritual and rhythm. As in the dance we learn, by constant repetition, to get over our self-consciousness and awkwardness, to become responsive, almost instinctively, to every movement and mood of our partner and gradually become free to let ourselves be carried along by the music; so in marriage, through the ritual recurrence of the erotic pattern – involving our mind as much as our body, our sensitivity as much as our nerves – we become spontaneous and graceful. Of course, spontaneity cannot be practised. It is as paradoxical to say 'thou shalt be spontaneous' as 'thou shalt love'.[11] Yet this is what Jesus says, and in marriage we may realize that the paradox simply expresses the tension by which we are kept alive: we cannot give what is demanded of us – our spontaneous love – unless it is again and again awakened in us. Yet our situation reminds us that just what we cannot give is demanded and that the demand is inextricably entangled with our desires. For not only do we want to be loved, but, even more, we want the other to keep alive our love and, in loving, to remain lovable.[12]

Marriage demands and promises *gracefulness*, that paradox of discipline and freedom, the shape and life of all worth while human achievements. To train us in gracefulness and make us spontaneous is the main purpose of marriage. All other purposes have to be made subservient to it – however much we hanker after 'order' and 'peace'. That purpose alone judges and justifies us in our marriage and is its most rigorous taskmaster. When we impose upon ourselves disciplines contradicting or evading the discipline of gracefulness, when we fall back on 'law and order', duty and responsibility, we exchange hope for the counsel of despair, we sell our sincerity for less than a pot of porridge.*

Our modern world has become so graceless, largely because it lacks spontaneity. The structure of our technological society leaves little scope for its development, most occupations discourage it. Modern means of production are on the whole too far removed from the satisfaction of vital human needs, and the pressure of a dehumanized concept of industrial and economic efficiency makes itself felt even in the lives of those who are not directly involved in the technological process. In a society governed almost exclusively by impersonal and often inhuman considerations, marriage offers some of the few remaining chances to become human and humane.

In marriage I may discover how to become myself. I need not submit to external, mechanical demands. I may take off the mask of the civil servant, the shop assistant, the company director, shake off the constraint of the mill, office or workshop, the impersonal responsibility of the politician or the personnel manager. Here, contrary to commonly accepted

---

*The fact that many marriages degenerate into half-hearted togetherness which makes 'strange disciplines' imperative, does not permit the moralist to confront us with anything less than the discipline of joy. A marriage held together only by 'practical' considerations – even if they include children – is an impracticable marriage.

ideas, I may shed my *irresponsibility* – induced by the lack of opportunity for decision in my job or by decisions of no directly human consequence. Here I become responsive to and responsible for the intimate personal problems of other human beings which are the only problems that really matter.

Whether I am a scientist or a greengrocer, a committee lady or her charwoman, a maker of rockets or of pins, the fundamental human problems are the same: how to love and how to cope with the failure of love, how to adapt myself and how to deal with my frustrations, how to face sickness and death, my false and true desires, how to bring up my children. These problems are complex and searching and endless. They are the stuff comedies and tragedies are made of – and it is perhaps no accident that no satisfactory play or novel has yet been written about a factory, the running of a department store or an office. It is therefore of vital importance that we continually permit our changing and maturing marriage experiences to influence the choice and nature of our work, else the inhuman tendencies of our work will condition our marriage. The refusal to acknowledge the organic connexion between work and home will have to be paid for in terms of schizophrenia, neurosis, bitterness and frustration – perhaps of war and annihilation.

Possessions and Procreations

Marriage could teach us – more persuasively than the monastery – the place we should assign to our material possessions. Whatever helps us to become free and have more time for one another, whatever makes us grow and grow together in sympathy and sensibility, we should try to acquire – and help others to do the same. Anything that withholds us from one another, wastes our time, squanders our energy on ephemeral and sterile satisfactions, stands in the way of spontaneous intercourse, should be avoided or thrown out of the window. For what does it profit a man if he should be able to afford all the world's gadgets and lose his first love? An excessive desire for 'things' – to have or to happen – is an indication of a failure in love and life. Today none of us is immune from the insinuation that a man can be saved – at least from boredom – by the 'up-to-dateness' of his possessions or the multitude of his engagements. Most of us have more than we need and do more than is good for us. We are so much encumbered by many things that we have no time for that 'good part', the living of our lives.[13]

(It is generally agreed that suffering and frustration cannot be kept at bay by a bank account or a television set, yet millions are mesmerized by the latter 'encumbrance' and fritter away their freedom in front of the flickering screen with the unexpressed hope that their unlived lives may be lived for them. Even if what they saw was good, it would still rob them of much of their freedom to experience for themselves, to express their lives. For the children, television destroys the mystery and imagination of childhood. For the middle aged it is an escape into artificial thrills and adventures which prevents them from facing their loss of zest for living. For the old – to whom, we are told, this invention has brought great blessings and consolation – it has become the screen that bars the view to a final assessment of their lives and cheats them and us of the final fruit of wisdom. There comes a time when we should meditate on the meaning and 'end' of life. Death cannot be entertained away.)

In marriage we may understand why we cannot serve God and mammon, why love and possessiveness are mutually exclusive, and why a recovery of the true meaning of *asceticism*[14] could be of great importance for our gadget-ridden world. We are too preoccupied with the tangible and ponderable and forget that the most hopeful things in life are intangible and imponderable. Possessions are the epitome of what can be measured – and possessiveness is the attempt to turn what cannot be possessed into a possession – and they have a tendency, by reason of their ponderousness, to become for us the measure of what is real, secure and true. Yet there is a certain hopelessness about things, a heaviness that has little to do with the law of gravitation. They make us less flexible and clutter up our minds even more than our rooms. They are a strain on nerves as well as muscles, they possess us as much as we possess them.[15] Our possessions infect us with their lifeless existence. To be able to do without much that is nowadays taken for granted, for the sake of lightness and gracefulness, for the sake of 'treasures in heaven', is a necessary step towards the full life.

Love is dynamic and restive and can find satisfaction only in what is restless and unpredictable.* It is not a problem – not even a sex-problem – that needs to be answered, but a drama that wants to be acted, a plot or a plant that wants to unfold. Love – and this may well be the touchstone of its truth – wants to beget and to give birth, it craves, as already Diotima knew, for immortality. It is not interested in things that have to be pushed about and dusted, but in things that have life in themselves, that grow and compel us to grow with them: in children. But not necessarily children of the flesh.† Love longs to bear fruit, while our age is preoccupied almost exclusively with works and tries to make a work even of childbearing. To bear fruit means to let something grow spontaneously and inevitably out of the very centre of our living and loving: it may be as intangible as joy, as overwhelming as the St Matthew Passion, as ponderous as a cathedral, as light as a new insight, it may be a baby. Whatever it is, it is something that increases us, intensifies our awareness, reproduces, recreates and resembles us and absorbs our best energies, as the plum

* I am convinced that much hysteria is due to the fact that our lives – including our wives, husbands and children – have become too predictable. The old instinct of worry has nothing to feed on and feeds on itself.

† Young couples of great sensibility may sometimes feel themselves called into the propagation of children which are not of the flesh, but suffer from a bad conscience, because they have grown up in a society which still takes the consequences of sexual intercourse for granted, although there is no longer any compelling reason for doing so. I think they ought to be encouraged in their desire to bear strange fruit – e.g. in art, education, social or cultural work – for there is a danger that in our concentration on life as such we forget the propagation – the begetting and bearing – of those values and insights without which life is not worth living and for which children of flesh and blood often do not leave us time.

the sap from the tree, to become food and sweetness: food for thought, for appreciation, for a new love – as no work can ever be.

CHAPTER FOUR

The Promise of Wholeness and Loveliness

CREATIVITY

WE are incorrigible anthropomorphists. What we cannot transmute into configurations pleasing to touch or smell, sight or hearing, logic or dream, does not captivate us. We can grasp the universe only by means of those patterns of logic and intuitions which grew out of the rhythm and motions and harmonies of dance and music, poetry and drama, painting and sculpture, which, in turn, grew out of the rhythm of breathing and lovemaking and the discipline of primitive magic and craftsmanship. We see the universe in our image and there is no reason to assume that another creature would see in it anything remotely resembling our vision. Goethe says that the eye could not perceive the sun if it were not 'sun-like'. We may go one step further and add* that the sun could not be seen by us as we actually see it, if it were not in some way 'eye-like'.

Our thoughts and senses, motions and emotions, have imposed upon the universe a shape that enables us to recognize ourselves in it, to cope with it and to accept it as a home and a challenge. This archetypal effort which is dimly repeated by every child is fundamentally an aesthetic labour, an erotic creation. The result is *beauty* which strikes us as 'truth' when it is useful and as beautiful when it is life-enhancing – and Keats' 'Beauty is truth, truth beauty' may be nearer the metaphysical bone than we had thought.

The discipline of beauty humanizes the world we live in and humanizes us by persuading us of the 'truth' we discover in

*I do not want to maintain that our senses had not first been conditioned by the universe of our experience. All I want to say is that this conditioning was, as far as we can judge, a unique process and need not have led logically or inevitably to the kind of sensibility which is now, for better and for worse, the glass through which we see – darkly or not so darkly according to our taste and expectation.

the patterns we have imposed. Since 'truth' can be seen as an aspect of beauty, it is understandable that it should become most persuasive, alive and relevant, when it strikes us as beautiful, graceful and hopeful.[1] As long as 'truth' lacks gracefulness, it has not yet attained its full humanizing power, it is still immature, not yet 'realized'*. The 'realization' of truth-beauty I call *incarnation*, and it is achieved – however transitorily – whenever the truth touches us as self-authenticating and adequate and the beauty as intimation and revelation. Nothing can preserve us from the abstractions of intellectualism, moralism and aestheticism, from the divorce between the 'is' and the 'ought', duty and love, except the continued effort to achieve incarnation, to discover and recover the truth that charms and the beauty that compels.

If the striving after beauty is the human quest *par excellence*, the quest by reason of which we have become and remain man, it is important to make this truth persuasive. For, unfortunately, our understanding of beauty is deeply coloured by our puritanical, utilitarian, industrial heritage. Far from seeing beauty as our supreme achievement and task, the revelation of our stature, we think of it as luxury, indulgence, as something not vitally necessary for the business of living. 'Seek first all things, and the kingdom will be added unto you' is an axiom few of us dare to contradict in word or deed. So let us have a look at the artist, the wrestler with beauty and truth, and see whether his work reveals to us something that is essential, necessary to our life.

THE ARTIST

1. Beauty as Transfiguration

Beauty, as many might admit, has nothing to do with prettiness, with making things smooth, nice and comfortable. It is never just a means of entertainment and relaxation. It is severe, searching, disturbing as well as joyous, frightening as well as invigorating.

---

*To 'realize' = to give reality as well as to apprehend clearly.

Beauty is most nearly itself – closest to its archetypal wrestling with chaos – when it takes up and *transfigures* what is in itself unlovely, or when it imposes on the inchoate outburst of joy the painful discipline of form and reflection. Most things of beauty – like most children – are born out of suffering which is part of the joy which bestows upon the gift the dimension of achievement. Beauty as the transfiguration of the human dilemma can be experienced most powerfully in the art of tragedy. In the *Oresteia*, for instance, one of the earliest and greatest works, Aeschylus succeeds, by his intense, sympathetic insight into the human heart, in transforming a sordid tale of family intrigue and vendetta into a drama of universal redemption. (The fact that we find it hard to see the Oresteia as a petty vendetta is the measure of his success.)* In *King Lear*, Shakespeare succeeds in reaffirming the dignity of a foolish old man, in the face of a nightmare of pitiless terror let loose largely by his own foolishness, and encourages us to believe that a man, even a foolish man, can remain or, rather, become a king, 'every inch a king', in spite of the combined heartlessness of men and nature. Ibsen in *Masterbuilder*, and *John Gabriel Borkmann*, even in *Hedda Gabler* or *The Wild Duck*, and Shakespeare in his tragedies, make us aware of the great possibilities of life by presenting to us people who tried, however inadequately, to 'realize' some of them. Chekhov in a very different manner gives us that awareness by letting us love and identify ourselves with the men and women who fail so pathetically and comically to 'realize' their lives. The tragic hero lives in his death, and his death is the judgement on his inadequate response to his situation. It is also his redemption, since he has endeavoured to make at least some kind of response. We are purged by participating vicariously in his movement towards a fuller 'realization'. This movement is so vital to our humanity that we can sympathize even with those heroes who – like Macbeth or Hedda – only succeed in making the altogether wrong response. Tragedy, by the discipline of

*Just as the fact that we no longer experience the sea as the beginning of shapeless terror and the mountains as haunts of demons, but appreciate both as beautiful, is a measure of our success.

beauty, awakens our sympathy with the lost, enables us to recognize our kinship with them. It lays open before us that fundamental structure of true morality, denied and hidden by most of our moralizing, which turns from the unlovely without any desire to transfigure it.

Another miracle of transfiguration can be seen in such paintings as the late self-portraits of Rembrandt, where the beauty is a pitiless and disciplined searching for the sheer, naked truth; or in the terrifying honesty of vision of a Breughel, a Goya, a Gruenewald, or a Picasso in his *Guernica*. Why should a naturalistic account of an execution, a crucifixion, strike us as beautiful? What is it that enabled Schubert to transmute his grief and misery into works like the 'Death and the Maiden' quartet or the '*Winterreise*'? What enabled Mozart to translate his despair into the 'Requiem'? How is it that even disgust and loathing can be changed into the stinging beauty of satire?

2. *Beauty as discipline*

Beauty is disciplined passion. Passion without discipline becomes destructive. Discipline without passion is senseless and can become equally destructive.*

Where passion and discipline are welded together in an act of creative energy, something hard, timeless and exhilarating is born. (This holds good in marriage and friendship – which are creative activities.) The more intense the experience, the more insistent the urge to delimit, circumscribe, tame. All art is symbolic, has the gracefulness of sustained power – like the movements of a tiger – suggesting the presence of untapped energy. Dante had to impose upon his burning vision the almost crippling discipline of the terza rima; and only the

*It is no accident that the actions of the over-organized, over-efficient, bureaucratic modern state sometimes reflect the barbaric outbursts of an Attila and Genghis Khan; that in the very heart of Europe a Hitler could arise; that the worst practices of his Gestapo were used by the paratroops of France; that the majority of over-industrialized Englishmen and Americans love to indulge in torture and sadism at least vicariously; that the prospect of nuclear war and the actual preparations for it leave our imagination almost undisturbed.

hardest material could brake and contain the passion of a Michelangelo. Music, the most Dionysian of human expressions, calls for an almost mathematical discipline. Where, as with Bach, supreme craftsmanship joins supreme spontaneity of inspiration, the result is a beauty of which one is not likely to tire.

Beauty is disciplined joy, the incarnation of gratefulness, the reminder that every achievement is a gift and that every gift wants to be 'achieved'. The great impressionists illustrate this point well. How lightly, joyfully and almost casually everything seems to be achieved here. Every canvas seems to be an effortless burst of praise, immortalizing anything from a sunset to an old pair of boots. Yet we know that behind that lightness of touch lies a lifetime of asceticism, a ruthless self-criticism, an almost despairing sincerity. Think of Monet wrestling with light for seventy years, of Degas triumphing over his failing sight, of Cézanne wrestling for years with an 'insignificant' hill and the atmosphere around it; and all of them bequeathing to us a moment immortalized, and teaching us to appreciate how many moments worth immortality there are in our life.

3. Beauty as Function

Finally, there is the beauty of function, of sheer adequacy, of simplicity, clarity, usefulness, the discipline of eliminating the superfluous and the superficial, of discovering creatively the unifying formula. That beauty is the tough discipline of the craftsman, the scientist, the mathematician and the engineer. A jet plane, a steel bridge, a modern block of apartment flats, a car, a machine or a factory, might perform a similar civilizing function as did the cathedral of old. On the other hand, it is almost always true that ugliness – except the ugliness of the trial and error stage – is the symptom of a moral as well as aesthetic breakdown. The fact that we still tolerate so much of the squalor inherited from the Industrial Revolution – lightless factories, monster mills, overcrowded slums, cramped schools – and even now perpetuate it, though in more hygienic forms – subtopian suburbs, unimaginative office blocks, vulgar hoardings and still more vulgar newspapers – is never simply a sign of aesthetic insensibility, but of moral and social decay.

JESUS THE ARTIST

Beauty as the discipline of transfiguration, function, joy and passion, gives to our love the clearest intimation of immortality. It gives body and substance to our infinite longings, feeds our hope and incites us to hope that our hope is not in vain. I therefore do not detract from the significance and weight of the words of Jesus when I say that they persuade us by their beauty and gracefulness. They incite our passions – as only beauty can. They lure us into new ventures and research, into strange company and stranger experiments – as only beauty does. They insinuate themselves until they become as teasingly self-explanatory, as hauntingly and irreducibly parabolical, as all true beauty.

Jesus reshaped the universe of our experience as in an act of supreme artistic creation: he recreated it in the image and proportions of man; transfigured it into a place where a man may feel at home, may live as in a father's house and feel responsible as for a father's house. He urges us to consider the world as an opportunity we may grasp and to trust that it will yield to our importunity. He makes our aspirations commensurate with the world and promises *nothing* to those of us who want less than everything.[2]

Like most great artists, Jesus does not talk about creation. He creates. Nor would he have thought of himself as an artist. He was nurtured by a tradition that did not really know the concept of art, that had not yet become self-conscious in respect of its aesthetic experience. He stood in the line of the prophets who considered themselves as slaves of a living truth which compelled them to speak – not as poets. (Yet there is no doubt that some of them in their single-minded obsession with 'truth' became great poets.)

It is therefore difficult to substantiate my understanding of Jesus as artist by direct quotations. The Fourth Gospel can sum up his teaching in the 'I am the way, the truth and the life', 'I am the true vine', etc. It cannot let him say 'I am the perfect beauty', largely because the Jews, still under the Second Commandment, had not learned to catch and eternalize the most obvious, the visible beauty. They had not yet isolated the idea of the beautiful. On the other hand there are the sayings concerning the 'glory' of Jesus and, above all, there is the Prologue to the Fourth Gospel, in which Jesus, the bringer of the word of God, of the word that *is* God, is identified with the Word that creates heaven and earth. We can, of course, understand that mythologically, assume a 'God' whom we already know and equate Jesus with him, talk of 'pre-existence' and the Trinity – although in doing this we go against the intention of the writer of the Fourth Gospel who says: 'No one has ever seen God', 'he who has seen *me* has seen the Father'. Or we can try to understand him existentially and discover in the process how transparent his Gospel becomes, how surprisingly modern and relevant.

Jesus is God, the author maintains, because he speaks the words that create all things, because he recreates and re-illuminates by his words the chaos and darkness into which whatever has been created continues to subside. Or, to put it the other way: when the words of Jesus begin to give purpose, scope and energy to our lives, when they remake us and we experience this as miraculous, then we begin to realize his beauty, his glory, we begin to appreciate his life as a parable, as revelation, and to acknowledge him as *our* God.[3] And as in our growing understanding of his words as 'life' and 'light' we fall ever more intensely in love with his 'glory'; we respond, like the beloved to the lover, convinced that he is unique, the 'only begotten, full of grace and truth', that 'apart from him we can do nothing' and that we had certainly not 'seen God' until he was revealed to us in the lover.[4]

There is no God but Jesus, says the author of John's Gospel,[5] because his words, more than any other words, build us up, refresh us, guide and gather us, resuscitate us, because they bring us life and the abundance of it – and we experience such abundance as beauty, as glory. He brings joy – and joy is response to loveliness – the joy that awakens the dead and makes them crave for eternity.[6] Beyond that, Jesus is seen as the moulder of his life. He shapes his own fate in obedience to his own words: he is not only willing to die for his vision, to give his life for the sake of life. We are made to see him as the man who passionately and creatively made his death, even the death of shame, into the consummation and intensification of his life and its purpose: 'I, when I am lifted up, will draw all men to myself.' He went into death as into something that re-affirmed his life, he used it to express and confirm his conviction that life – the life he loved, this death-bound life – is a parable, a work of art, if you like, and that as such it is indestructible. And the great 'I am' sayings insist that the 'I' is the profoundest of all parables.[7]

The author of the Fourth Gospel does not see Jesus as a hero who claims divinity – as the Greek hero might have done. He sees him as the visionary – the artist – who is absorbed and fulfilled by his vision. He is exclusively the revealer of what he has seen. He can do nothing except show what has been shown to him. He does not 'make himself', he is made by his vision. He has not chosen it, he is sent. We can come to his 'truth' only through his vision, and to him only when the vision has captivated us. But since Jesus is pre-eminently the artist of his own life, he can say that he and his vision are one, that he incarnates his vision, that he who has seen Jesus has seen the Father.[8]

The Fourth Gospel is an interpretation of the words of Jesus. It is an artistic recreation. I have chosen it, because the creativity of Jesus can be grasped best when his work is viewed as a whole, and this is what the author of this most incarnational of all the Gospels does. Let us now turn to the words – as recorded in the Synoptics – from which he drew such startling inferences.

Jesus teaches in parables. All his teaching is parabolic.[9] This is so of necessity, for his message is the expression of his conviction – or hope? or belief? – that this world is a parable, a symbol, a something which can only be described in a paradox: It is and is not self-contained; it points beyond itself towards something it already contains, and everything it contains points towards further possibilities and consummations. The world, like a parable, is a completed whole which nevertheless leaves us restless and hopeful. Jesus' teaching throughout can be understood as an elaboration of this insight. It tries to persuade us that everything, when looked at hopefully and with expectation, can become transparent, revelatory, teasing.

The overriding concept of this insight is the *kingdom*. It is like growth, desire, action to some purpose; like cheating, importuning, begging. It is within us, among us, near at hand, always before us. It is like harvest, producing new life and new seed. It is miraculous, mysterious, all-pervasive, commonplace. It is like a branching out, a deployment of all our talents, like a great party, like beauty worth more than everything a man possesses. It is like living unto death as if death were merely a bursting into life. The world *is* the kingdom, in as far as all these events do take place in it. It is only a parable of the kingdom, in as far as all these events can never be more than an intimation of a joy that craves for eternity. (*Eternal life* is the Johannine equivalent of the synoptic *kingdom*.) This explains the emphasis on movement into life not yet realized, on dying into life, on giving up everything for the sake of a new beginning; the stress on the lost: lost sheep, coin, son; the sinner, the outcast, the alien, the sheep without shepherd. For only those who love life so intensely that they expect more of it than it has yet given and much more of themselves than they have yet achieved; who feel lost, inadequate, 'sinners', can enter the kingdom – will understand the world as a parable. Jesus recreates us, becomes our 'saviour', when his words make life so poignantly desirable that we can no longer help seeing everything as a parable and promise of more life. For those that remain outside their spell, his words remain *only* parables, they cannot recreate, *save*. They cannot help us until they have captivated us by a gracefulness that needs no further justification.[10]

A closer look at one or two of his parables may help us to appreciate the creative artist whose material is the world.

Be not anxious about the future, for you cannot add a day to your life, look at the birds and the lilies, their carelessness and glory! Are you not worth more than many birds and flowers?

Jesus does not believe we should or could live like ravens or lilies. But he incites us to live as if this world were a place where, if we single-mindedly desired to grow into completion, into our glory, like the lilies, we shall be protected, cared for and find fulfilment. Or rather – for we should remember what Jesus suffered for his 'as if' – we shall no longer be afraid of them who only kill the body but cannot touch the life that craves for and promises 'eternity'. We shall only fear that which destroys the spontaneity without which life is not worth living, is 'uneternal' life. (It may be worth adding here that the joy Jesus offers is not to be mistaken for happiness. It is something we cannot have without much unhappiness, something that is tested and enhanced by disappointment. For its sake we are not afraid to have our heart broken.)

The story of the Prodigal Son is a many-faceted parable. Here I want to point out the skill with which Jesus manipulates our emotions and engages our sentimentality. The father in the story is not God. (If Jesus had presupposed God and our knowledge of him in that fashion, there would have been no need for revelation and Jesus would have been reduced to the stature of a Bunyan.) The father is a bit of a dotard who has apparently not succeeded in making a very good job of either of his two sons. One wants to leave him as soon as he may. The other one, although he stays on, has never learned to love him enough to enjoy being with him. There is much about the old man that is left completely unexplained. His behaviour on the occasion of the younger son's return would have startled not only the prodigal but the hearers of the story. Surely, they would have felt, a father should not behave with so little dignity! But this precisely is one of the points of the tale. It stirs our sentimentality, our hope, by moving us against our better judgement. Although the old man's actions seem to leave much to be desired and we are tempted to judge him rather harshly, we cannot help being touched by his behaviour – and feel disgusted with the elder son who is not equally touched. Over and above this – and this is Jesus' artistry – his handling of the story intrigues our sentiment, our innate desire for correspondences. It makes us wonder whether the great unknown which stands over against us and leaves so much to be desired and explained, may not be after all a little like such a father, and our life – so often futile and even disgusting in our own sight – such a homecoming. Jesus seems to have lived as if he had been convinced by his parable.

Finally, the story of the Wicked Servant. It does not help to think of the king as God – though the writer of the First Gospel most likely did – and of the servant as the sinner who does not forgive them that sin against him. The main character is the servant, not the king. He is the man who realizes suddenly that he has frittered away more than he can hope to repay – that his days do not add up to a sum which even distantly approaches his expectation, that the day will come when all his days will add up to exactly nothing. There is nothing he can do about it except fall down and mumble the meaningless words: 'Have patience and I will repay you all.' It is important to realize that the words are meaningless in as far as they promise the impossible. They are intensely meaningful in that they express our impossible hope: to be given another chance. Now the teasing begins: Suppose there is another chance. It would involve One to give it; most likely – if it is likely at all – the One who has given us the first chance. But if there is such a One, then we are 'responsible', answerable, we have frittered away what was not ours. We are worse than failures, we are 'sinners', we are guilty. Or, to turn the teasing into modern words: Our hope for a second chance depends on our admission – at least to ourselves – that we are responsible for our lives and for the world we live in, that our failings are not failures – which add up to the ultimate failure of death – but guilt which can be forgiven in the sense that we can be given another chance, because the failing was not inevitable. To understand oneself as a failure leads to despondency. To understand oneself as a 'sinner' makes hopeful. For the more intensely I realize my responsibility, the more I shall long for the return of the lost opportunity – and the ultimately lost opportunity is life itself. The parable does not end there. It would have remained innerworldly, that is otherworldly, and so unparabolic. The proof of my desire for another chance lies in my eagerness to give it. The restoring of lost opportunities to those who lost them concerning me, will feed my conviction – so the words of this parable promise – that the ultimate meaning and revelation of life is such restoration.

If we look at the words of Jesus in this way, we understand why we cannot ask whether he was right or wrong – just as it is meaningless to ask whether Michelangelo's picture of the Last Judgement is a true copy of the 'real thing', or whether Einstein's space is a true description of space 'as it really is'. All we may ask – and cannot help asking – is whether Jesus' vision is significant for us, whether it gives our lives significance and makes the world appear significant to us. But significance is an aesthetic experience. Only what we can understand as beautiful, rounded, coherent, or as pressing towards completion, cohesion, beauty, teases us by intimations of significance. (This holds true in science as well as in art.) So the words of Jesus cannot be measured against a metaphysical certainty or our present day scientific grasp of the world. We have to let them speak to us as directly as a drama, a picture, a symphony, the beauty of a girl, a mathematical solution, a physical theory. As we listen to them, they may or may not grow in significance. But nothing can convince us of their 'truth', their beauty, except they themselves, as they become for us an adequate interpretation of experience and an adequate guide to the art of living and loving. In other words: when their interpretation makes us see the world as beautiful and life as desirable.

LOSS OF WHOLENESS

It is therefore surprising how often the moralist has neglected to discuss the formative power of beauty and the creative activities which sharpen our appreciation of it. Plato seems to have remained the only one among the great who was convinced of the profound influence of beauty on the shaping of a man's life. An exploration of the conditions that enable man to grow in imagination and sensibility should be a vital aspect of any moral inquiry. There were times when that seems to have been understood. The Athens of Pericles comes to mind and perhaps the Florence of the Medici. But beauty cannot be recovered. For beauty is alive, the formulation of a living experience, changing with the changing times which it reflects and transfigures. It expresses our striving after wholeness and our partial success.

The failure to understand beauty as the demand for wholeness and health may be responsible for the fragmentation of our experience and life. We are not – like the lilies – shaped by an inevitable unfolding of our innate capacities, but largely by outward routine and circumstances. Away from his work, from the chores of house and car and garden, modern man is pathetically at sea and at the mercy of many voices promising 'salvation', 'distraction from distraction by distraction'. Like the daily paper, his life is a jumble of impressions, vicarious experiences and chatter. His responses are almost entirely conditioned by the 'mechanical' requirements of his situation. He does not say to mountains, 'be moved into the sea'. He does not know how to grow in heart and mind and tenderness; he wants to 'get on'. He does not seek the fulness of life but a higher income, not joy but happiness. (He often finds what he seeks.) He does not long to become himself, but to be acceptable in the eyes of his neighbours and superiors. 'Blessed are you when all men speak well of you and heap honour upon you.' He does not want to think and feel, but to conform, to find without seeking, to be answered without asking. He does not want to commit himself, wants to be left in peace, even at the price of war. He is suspicious of the absolute compulsion of an inner purpose and clings with pride to the routine demands of his position. He does not think of himself as the centre of a very particular world he has to humanize and make responsive to his aspiration – 'all things are possible to him who believes' – but feels at the mercy of an impersonal and comfortable necessity. Unfortunately this does not correspond to the organic necessity of life. So we feel frustrated and escape from the consciousness of our fragmentation into mechanical entertainment, observance, ritual and prayer, which fragments us even more.*

Some astronomers try to explain the universe as the result of a cosmic explosion hurtling a myriad worlds away from each other at ever increasing velocity. It would be interesting to know in how far they were influenced in forming their theory by the psychological realities of our age. 'Things fly apart, the centre will not hold.'[11] (Compare the accelerating process of specialization in fields as varied as the study of physics, theology or Shakespeare.) Do we accept this state of affairs as fate or challenge? Do we resign ourselves to it as inevitable – trying to find a niche for our life and prejudices in one of the hurtling worlds – or do we feel called to create a new *uni*verse?

INTIMATIONS AND RETURN

The world is too much with us and might easily persuade us to accept fragmentation as our modern condition, if it were not for those haunting experiences which make us aware of another power at work in us. I am thinking of those recurring moments that compel us to discern or, at least, to yearn for, a meaning and a pattern, an organic unfolding of 'eternity'. We suddenly find ourselves absorbed, pulled together, directed and justified. We do not fret. We want nothing beyond what we have and what is promised in what we have. We desire nothing except the life we live, only more of it. A real encounter, an unreserved response and surrender, the contemplation of a thing or a face or an idea, the act of creation or procreation or perfect receptivity when 'you are the music while the music lasts',[12] are experiences which cannot be exorcised however fleeting and unproductive they may be. Measured in terms of light years and technical efficiency, they are insignificant. But it is equally true that light years and the

*Puritanism and libertarianism, aestheticism and vulgarity, pure scholarship and pure opinionating, are equally inadequate responses to the almost forgotten promise of wholeness.

wonders of technology are insignificant when measured against those experiences. For their sake, if only we had the courage and the faith, we would gladly give all.

'What does it profit a man to gain the whole world and forfeit his life?' is not a religious statement. It is an existential fact and we all know it. But if we look at the pearl of great price too long, we are not likely to give for it all we have. If we return once too often to the field with the forgotten treasure, we are likely to be discovered before we have decided on the purchase – and we shall try to persuade ourselves afterwards that we have dealt wisely.

Beauty, whether it lures us into creation or procreation, into embracing a person or a task, requires committal. We have to base vital decisions on very inconclusive evidence, and all we can ever know is that we shall make a mess of our furrow, if we look back after having put our hand to the plough. The decision to heed the intimation is all the more difficult, since we are deeply involved in the process of dehumanization. We have got used to taking the priority of peripheral problems over the actual business of living for granted. The vast technological superstructure fascinates us by the tidiness of its complexity, by its clear-cut objectives. It has become a refuge from the real tasks of living. But creation, like birth, is untidy, unpredictable, its consequences cannot be contained. They may master us and change us and we shall not know into what until it has happened. (Of course, the machine, too, changes us. But it is subtler than our children and leaves us under the illusion that we are the master.)

Furthermore, we are afraid to turn from the oppressively tangible securities of the 'machine', of mammon, to the elusive – perhaps illusive – moments when our life seemed justified, rounded and open, but also profoundly insecure – for such moments are not at our bidding.[13] We have waited too long for such a turning to be easy. Yet I am convinced that nothing except the reactivated desire to look first for the *kingdom*, to become, like the lilies, a joy to oneself and others, to be the liver of one's life, can save us from final disintegration. Life presses towards fruit, seed-bearing fruit; and by creativity, I understand the effort to channel all our life-juices into something that expresses us and yet has life in itself.

The movement beauty requires will not necessarily take us into the desert, it need not lead to iconoclasm or return to the handloom or the potter's wheel – although it might. It is certainly not a turning away from this world, an escape into obscurantism or utopianism. It is a wrestling with the most earthy realities of the present situation. But it is a decisive turning – 'costing no less than everything'[14] – from the peripheral to the centre, from the slavery of sheer proliferation to the mystery of growth.

The cost is great, because creation needs much time. (The machine leaves us little.) It takes us into many culs-de-sac and sucks its best nourishment out of failure and heartbreak. But careers are straight and lubricated and cannot tolerate the waywardness of gestation. Creativity grows out of much meditation, introspection, chasing of moods and changes of mind; out of intense efforts to gain sympathetic insights into men and things. The modern corporation – whether of state or church, of political party or industry – is happiest with those who do not think too much, do not change their mind, and do not urge others to change it. In other words: those that want to follow the 'vision', the 'call', the intimation, must be ready to be considered cranks, failures and useless by their fellow men – and to accept the fact that they will often look upon themselves as such.[15]

As our creative energies continue to shrivel, two consequences will ensue: first, the world will become progressively denuded and inhuman. We shall no longer see it in our own image and shall end by having no image of ourselves. Our affections will become tied to emptiness, death and horror. Secondly, as we forget to fulfil the function of our life, to bring forth fruit, we shall gradually lose the capacity to understand growth, the mother of all parables. The world of the spirit will become two-dimensional and opaque – as a television screen – and we shall be unable to understand it – and ourselves – as a parable. We shall have become irretrievably 'uneternal'.[16]

THE PROMISE OF CREATIVITY

Creativity is the 'realization' of life, of our uniqueness. In creative action we become aware of the strange interplay between power and impotence, freedom and necessity, commandment and grace, as of the reality of our human condition. Here we are compelled to acknowledge our limitations – neither too late nor too early, if we are really creative – and to understand them as challenge and promise. *This* we can do. *That* we cannot do yet, although we would love to. But 'all things are possible to him who believes.'

Until beauty has seduced us into taking up many labours we cannot hope to complete in our time and strength, we shall not know the meaning of the hope which is not a utopian or religious delusion. We must have been tempted to cope with many tasks beyond our power, before we can realize that there is a faith distinct from credulity. We must have been lured into desiring to give more than we can possibly give, before we can understand the meaning of love which is more than a mutual indulgence.[17]

In every creative wrestling with men or things we arrive at the point where the very intensity of our desire for more seems to mock us and makes us despair. This is the moment of 'forgiveness', of longing for 'another chance', the moment when the promise of life and the kingdom may become more than a doctrinal formulation: a frightening, bracing, clear-cut hope. Creativity brings joy and frustration, it insists on pushing me to the point where my desire to go further is as great as my inability to 'realize' it. Here I meet myself and despair and here alone I cannot help hoping against despair that what is impossible may be possible after all. The words of Jesus seduce me to go to that extremity, because there is no other way of finding out whether I hope. (Religion, christian or non-christian, presents man with the 'promise' before he has arrived at the place where it has become meaningful to him. In this way the promise becomes dogma, love becomes charity and men begin to believe in creeds.)

Creative work is definite: the nurturing of this child, the moulding of this stone, the tackling of a unique task. Yet, although the glory of all creativity is its concreteness, it is equally true that whatever we tackle creatively leaves us ultimately unsatisfied and restive. In dealing with men or things, we are never justified by what we have done – however lovely it may be – but by what we have not yet achieved but have been trained for in our work. In short: we have never done. We can only hope that what we have done will be fruit and bear seed.

On the other hand, I cannot help hoping that the seed-bearing fruit will be the consummation of a unique existence: my life, that my life will be fruit. Here again the words of Jesus prick and tickle.[18] They tempt me to live as if there were always life. They urge me to admit that I cannot think of life except as *my* life and to live *my* life as if it would always be mine. And my life is this most definite, singular, circumscribed something I am in the process of becoming in my creative responses and activities. (cf. our *True Deceivers*, chapter three.)

CHAPTER FIVE

The Promise of The Neighbour

ACCORDING to my experience, I find at the centre of my life not 'something' but 'someone' – my wife or husband, child, friend, parent, hero – someone I have or have lost. I am moved, in the last resort, not by a 'machine', a concept, ideology which I can master, but by an 'other' to whom I can or want to surrender, because his beauty – of body, mind or spirit – has mastered me. Our profoundest craving, in spite of all the apparent evidence to the contrary, is not for power but to be overpowered. And, being incorrigible anthropomorphists, it may well be that we become less than human when we let ourselves be overpowered by anything less than a man. Jesus confirms our experience and craving and makes them absolute: 'He who has seen me,' he says to his friends, 'has seen God. Why, having seen me, do you still ask for more?'[1]

The words of Jesus continue to tease us with the promise of a neighbour who has what we need, or rather with the challenge to find what we need in our neighbour. Nothing, of course, can move us to see our neighbour in such hopeful light, except our neighbour's own loveliness. But we can be helped to find and appreciate it by (1) *creative activity* which makes us raw and open to the world, training and expanding our *imagination and sensibility*, (2) *the words of Jesus*.

IMAGINATION AND MY NEIGHBOUR

a) Creativity needs the neighbour

He inspires me directly by his beauty, his thoughts, his complexity and opacity. He becomes the subject of my concern or meditation, a character in my novel or simply my gossip, a sitter for a portrait, a partner in discussion or lovemaking. Or he inspires me indirectly by his mere presence or his comments, by my expectation of his applause.

I need my neighbour, because he is the very *raison d'être* of my creativity: of my attempt to make known to the 'other' what I fear he might miss. Poets, playwrights, actors, musicians want to be *heard* – and so do lovers, wives, children and friends.

Our attempts at creativity and communication give body and substance to our togetherness. Where we have little to share or exchange, where creativity – whether the simple contemplation of the peasant or the pregnant brooding of a new Shakespeare – fails, human togetherness becomes barren. When we have no more to say or convey to each other, are no longer news and good news to each other, we are not neighbours – though a marriage vow bind us.

In some respects, the artist could be the epitome of a neighbour: he is the bringer of new light, the revealer of new dimensions, the midwife of our sensibilities, the herald of good news. Our attitude to the artist may reveal our attitude to our neighbour in general. Take the modern artist. His plight is almost desperate. Most men make no effort to understand him but are most willing to condemn him without any effort. A little coterie fawns on him, flatters his vanity, adores him and so corrupts him most insidiously. To remain true to his vision and himself between the indifference of the many and the adulation of the few, the artist of today requires a kind of courage which does not often go together with fine sensitivity.

The artist is a visionary. The meaninglessness and purposelessness of our society will impress themselves more strongly on him than on ordinary mortals and may lead him to despair – provided his sincerity is stronger than his love of success. To defend himself against too much heartbreak he is inclined to retire into a private – idiotic – universe, which, almost by definition is the contradiction of creativity. The artist's retirement robs us of what is best in our society and withdraws the means of renewal. We may blame the artist for not having greater faith in the possibility of renewal – for example in his art. But the fact that he has lost his faith is a sign that we, his neighbours, have lost faith in him, our neighbour.[2]

b) Love your neighbour as you love yourself

It takes a lifetime to come to know another person and the knowledge is not gained once and for all, but by continuous, adventurous adaptation. Every situation calls for a new response and every response creates a unique situation. But in this responsiveness I do not only come to know the other one, I come to know myself. All my essential knowledge of myself consists of my experience and use of my responses and responsibilities. I know myself as this father, husband, friend, member of this club, party, village, nation. (When I try to extricate myself from my responsibilities and retire into privacy or mysticism, my knowledge of myself becomes increasingly uncertain. In that we all avoid many of our responsibilities, we all are largely uncertain of ourselves.)

We begin to have a true insight into the stature of others when we realize that *they* know themselves only as similar centres of responsiveness and responsibilities. Unfortunately, I have neither the imagination, nor the energy, nor the sympathy to experience my neighbours' lives like that. It is therefore all the more important to remember that this is how they do, in fact, experience them. Whatever I do to my neighbour, or leave undone, I do to or withhold from one who in essentials is like myself, whom I can love – if I love at all – only as I love myself.[3] I shall want to do to him what I wish him to do for me. What I do to the 'other', I do to him as a son of his parents, a husband of his wife, a friend of his friends. Any action which takes him for less would clearly be inhuman.

I shall not fully appreciate the mystery of my ability to say 'I', until I have been awed by the realization that this precisely is the mystery of the 'other'. I shall not be able to love myself, until I come to love my neighbour as a 'myself'. The two are one. If I hate another, I cannot love myself, I can only hate myself. If I do not trust my neighbour, it shows that fundamentally I do not trust myself. If I am afraid of my neighbour, I should realize that there is much in me of which I am afraid and of which he has every reason to be afraid. I am most clearsighted concerning those faults in him which need correction in myself.[4] I am dissatisfied with him, when I am dissatisfied with myself. For it is equally true to say that I cannot love my neighbour until I love myself. When I feel frustrated, I shall judge him and condemn him for thoughts, words and deeds I felt compelled to inhibit. In fact, I shall loathe my neighbour as myself. When I feel insignificant, the whole world will look insignificant to me. 'What a man sees in the world is only himself as he sees himself in the deep and honest privacy of his own heart.'* My attitude to my neighbour reveals what I am.

If all this be true, I shall recognize that my neighbour needs as much space, time and free energy for his creative development as I myself. The more I am aware of my own need, the more I shall realize his. The less he realizes what he is missing, the more it is my responsibility to make him realize it. I shall also recognize that whatever I do for my neighbour will have to be the outcome of a spontaneous, creative response. I have certainly missed him as a neighbour, I cannot help him, if my action is simply in obedience to the law, in conformity with a convention, if it is a spiritual reflex. This is not what I would want him to do to me. *I* desire to be accepted by him as this most peculiar 'I', in these most particular circumstances, and I cannot help him, until what I do is a creative response to the challenge and mystery of his singularity![5] (This is true of our relationships with individuals as well as of our dealings with groups, whether we teach a child or reorganize a nation.)

There is my neighbour: We may be sharing bed and board. We may meet in the street, at work, over the garden wall. We may know him only through newspapers, statistics, appeals for help. He wants us to turn to him with heart and mind and soul.[6] He wants to be known by me as I try to know myself. He wants my imagination, emotion and understanding to play around him and caress him. He wants to be made much of. He wants me to be there for him, wants me to become a promise of health and wholeness to him – and in turn desires to become such a promise to me. This is the challenge and

*Mark Twain, *Puddenhead Wilson*, Preface.

promise of my neighbour, never very whole-heartedly accepted or believed, never altogether forgotten.

The words of Jesus pinpoint this promise and challenge. Through them we are in touch with one who claims to be our neighbour, because he has done – so the words claim – what we should like to do for our neighbour: he has revealed – or created – a beauty that persuades us by its relevance; he has revealed a truth which tempts us by its gracefulness; he has transformed the world into a home where men can meet as neighbours, into a neighbourhood, where life is not worth living apart from our neighbour.

THE WORDS OF A NEIGHBOUR

a) *Jesus our neighbour**

'Today this scripture has been fulfilled in your hearing.'[7] The promise of the Law and the Prophets, the apocalyptic hopes of the Israelites – the epitome of all great expectations – have been fulfilled in this man, a man without a permanent address who has nothing to offer but himself, who, for reasons impenetrable to his hearers, has the courage to make the claim 'today ... fulfilled', 'I, your neighbour, am your hope'. 'The kingdom of God', the words imply, is our neighbour; is our world when it becomes a neighbourhood. The 'kingdom' is entered by way of a personal relationship, a very definite committal. The claim cannot be tested, unless it is first accepted – 'come and see'[8] – it cannot be proved until we allow it to make fools of us.[9] The first hearers were aware of the 'graciousness of his words'. They were touched, they 'wondered', they 'spoke well of him' – they would have liked to believe. But 'is not this Joseph's son', one of us. What can you expect of one of us – of us? How can one of us be the fulfilment of our deepest longings? He is making fools of us! –

---

* The following does not attempt an exhaustive exegesis of the words quoted. It simply tries to show in how far the Gospel story illuminates the particular aspect of our inquiry. On the whole I shall follow – rather arbitrarily – the order of Luke.

We fail to understand the claim of Jesus, when we feel the need to reinforce it by pious or doctrinal considerations and try to divest it of the offensiveness it had for the first hearers: 'They led him to the brow of the hill ... that they might throw him down headlong'.

The claim 'I am he' or simply 'I am', puts our neighbour into the place we had preserved for those beatific visions that were meant to sweeten our apprehensions of death. Now we are told the 'kingdom' is near, here. It is our neighbour and demands no less than a complete reversal of our values and expectations. To receive the 'kingdom' in our neighbour, to acknowledge him as our 'kingdom', necessitates a complete change. 'New wine must be put into new wineskins.' All purely religious observances can be forgotten, when our neighbour, our 'bridegroom', is with us. When our neighbour inspires us with the hope with which the bridegroom is supposed to inspire the bride, there is no further need of ceremony and ritual. When love has renewed us, the allegory of renewal becomes superfluous.[10]

We are renewed by the realization of our neighbour's lovableness: the woman who comes to wash Jesus' feet with her tears has been a sinner. She has lived on love. Now she loves. She has been captured by a beauty which makes her see everything that went before as ugly. It is interesting to note that Jesus does not at first speak directly to her. 'Her sins are forgiven' he says about her. He does not proclaim absolution, he states a fact. He does not do anything – least of all 'forgiving sins' as if it was something one could 'do'. He acknowledges a state of affairs. The woman has found someone who has given her life a new direction. At least for the time being – and no human renewal is permanent – love has transfigured her. That is her forgiveness![11]

The Transfiguration Story is an attempt to describe the moment when our friend dazzles us by an intimation of a glory we had not suspected, when he seems to become transparent, when we realize that 'there is more to him than meets the eye'. Many of us have experienced such moments of transfiguration and been tempted – like Peter – to preserve them, to take

them out of the flux of time, to give them a religious or senti-
mental eternity. But the glory revealed in those moments is
not meant to be preserved. It cannot be re-experienced
through the recreation of the conditions in which it once
occurred or through a ritual repetition. It comes unexpectedly,
like joy, and, like joy, it wants to be shared. It wants to be
taken to those who for lack of a neighbour are possessed by
demons. The moment of transfiguration reminds us that we
should not expect a greater fulfilment than that which we find
through our friend – that we, too, may become such a transfigured neighbour.[12]

There is no sign by which our neighbour can legitimize
himself. He *is* the sign.[13] He challenges us by his presence, and
if that does not make us realize our condition, nothing else
will. 'Neither will they be convinced if someone should rise
from the dead', was the disconcerting answer to the man who
had ignored the presence of his neighbour at his own gate.[14]
There is no need to look for our neighbour anxiously, he is in
the midst of us.[15] I am able to love him when I trust him to
help me in difficulties, when I become convinced that he
could love me – as Jesus loved his friends – that I need him
more than anything I possess.[16]

b) *The promise of the neighbour*

The words of Jesus also explicate the promise we may expect
from our neighbour. In a true meeting we find health, completion, 'salvation'. Our legs become useful, their use pur-
poseful, when there is someone they can take us to and someone to send us out. Our withered hand becomes restored, when
it finds another hand to shake. Our eyes are opened when
we see our neighbour as neighbour.[17] We are cleansed
when we are met, when the isolation caused by our 'unclean-
ness' is broken by the readiness of the other one to be with us.
The demonic obsession of loneliness, self-centredness, possessiveness, can be driven out by the courage of my neighbour
who is ready to face me, the egoist, the idiot, the madman.
Such healing is worth thousands of pigs, the possessions of a
whole village.[18]

But the promise remains abstract, a dogmatic statement, until our eyes *have* been opened to see it, our hands unwithered to grasp it, our bodies 'raised' to live it. It remains a non-committal and religious promise, as long as it does not become for us what we most desire, the pearl of great price, worth more to us than all we have. And what we are promised is not an idyllic, but a full, complex relationship that is going to involve us in many troubles most of all with our own family.[19] Such a relationship does not give peace as the world understands it, for the neighbour breaks through the barriers of family, tribe, class, race, nation, party, club, etc., which are often no more than an extension of our self-centredness. (Even the rich man who had neglected his neighbour at the gate showed a laudable concern for his brothers.)

Our moral and religious teaching makes it hard for us to understand the promise. We teach our children in the nursery to 'love their neighbour' to be 'good Samaritans'. We make them understand love as duty, goodness as a rather unpleasant task, and any feeling of animosity or pugnaciousness as something wicked. (Church and state, industrial factions and political parties will make use of the suppressed animosities later on.) Such teaching often destroys the possibility of a real relationship more effectively than any open expression of our natural feelings of irritation. A real struggle can be transfigured, indifference cannot. Sometimes our neighbour can impress his reality upon us more strongly as an enemy than as a something one is bound to love. And unless we recognize his 'reality' as beautiful, our love will be pharisaical and sham.

In the light of the words of Jesus, most modern neighbourliness is revealed as sham. It is based on mutual indulgence, not on great expectations. Our law-abiding humility and toleration is not harmless. It compels us to bottle up our irritation; and 'wrath' not 'told' leads to boredom, and boredom to loathing which we do not permit ourselves to admit. This suppressed loathing must find someone to fasten on, and so it creates the 'enemy', the 'criminal', the unlovely, the neighbour of Kafka's tale. On the other hand, I believe that the original irritation is due to a misunderstanding of the christian promise: it arises from false expectations. We do not expect much, we expect 'too much' of our neighbour.[20] We expect him – or her – to bring us peace which does not pass our understanding, to make us happy, to keep us entertained, comfortable, wealthy. Jesus tells us that if we expect such things from our fellow men, we shall be disappointed[21] – no matter whether we get or do not get what we wanted.* Jesus promises us the kind of life in which we shall always be glad of a neighbour, not the life in which he becomes a luxury.[22] More, he tries to persuade us that a life which no longer depends on a neighbour, is no longer life[23] – Our neighbour does not limit or cramp our expectations, but gives shape to them – a human shape.

There remains the problem of unloveliness. We feel it would be easy to love a neighbour like Jesus, he would appear so obviously promising. But what are we to do about the people in whom we see no beauty? *First*, it may be worth remembering that at the end of his short missionary activity, Jesus had few followers. The great majority of his contemporaries seem to have found little beauty in him, and his best friends – at least after his arrest – little hopefulness. It cannot have been as easy to recognize Jesus' beauty as two thousand years of pious painting and teaching have made us imagine. Our unlovely neighbour, therefore, teases us with the possibility of a most striking loveliness for which, at the moment, we simply have no eye.

Secondly, my neighbour's unloveliness may be the consequence of my unneighbourliness.[24] My society which is the outward and visible sign of my inner attitude has made him ugly. His ugliness is my workmanship, certainly 'ours', it is the reflection of myself. *Thirdly*, it cannot always be assumed that my neighbour will have eyes for all the loveliness of which I am aware in myself. In spite of this I crave for his appreciation, and this craving should make me realize his need.

*Our modern entertainment industry – this it has in common with religion – lives on raising super-human, that is inhuman, or death-bound, hopes. Such hopes cannot find fulfilment and drive us back to the place where they were first raised. They are 'opium hopes'.

Yet not even these considerations can make the unlovely lovely, and to pretend that 'evil' is 'good' is, according to the words of Jesus, the one sin that cannot be forgiven, it is the pharisaical sin *par excellence*.[25] But my love will remain pharisaical love – sometimes called 'agape' – as long as I find no form of loveliness. I shall continue to do what I hate doing and hate myself for doing it and my neighbour who makes me do it. Who can deliver me, wretched man that I am![26]

The words of Jesus create a vision for us in which I see myself and my neighbour not so much as equally 'sinners', but as equally on the way to a yet far distant fulfilment. But the very words which remove the goal so far from my grasp, give nagging power to the hope that I can reach it.[27] The words make my hope inevitable and pathetic. They help me to see myself, as well as the greatest saint and the greatest sinner, as essentially pathetic – and pathos is the profoundest beauty. Man, stretching his great hope beyond the confines of this life, living against death, dying for life, is the most pathetic and the most invigorating spectacle. 'I, when I shall be lifted up, will draw all man to myself.' When we begin to see men in their pathos, their never quite broken glory, we shall begin to love them spontaneously.

CHAPTER SIX

The Promise of the City

DEUS IN MACHINA

FOR so long now that we hardly remember that it has not always been quite like this, the economic process has been treated as a vast automaton, a self-directing machine. Men are mere adjuncts, at best – if they are politicians or economists – mechanics who do the necessary repairs. In the ordinary economic textbook man does not count, except as 'supplier and demander', the marginal imponderable, the 'human element' which tends to upset our otherwise perfect calculations. Even in the welfare state we are not taken seriously as men and women, but as a function or a liability, as employers or employees, producers and consumers, receivers of welfare food or old age pensions. Life itself is thought of as a function of the economic process. The 'machine' has persuaded and charmed us. It has long since taken us past the point where we let it produce what we want, into the limitless territory where we become conditioned to want what it produces.

For instance: consider a modern newspaper. To set up the printing presses and keep them going, to break into the mass market and stay there, is an exceedingly costly business. Therefore, once the process has been started, it has to be kept going day by day. The question whether the editors, the leader writers, the reporters and feature writers, have anything worth while to say, whether the news is worth reporting, becomes completely irrelevant. So many pages have to be filled every day, so many million copies sold. Nothing else matters. If it is assumed that rubbish sells better than truth, then rubbish it will be. The truth would force us out of circulation – the one contingency not to be countenanced until more solidly economic factors make it actual.

Or take a television network. Once the millions have been

spent on its construction and administration, it becomes part of a necessity to which we have to conform. So many hours a week have to be filled somehow. We are not to consider whether there is enough creative intelligence available to fill those hours intelligently, or ask whether it is good for men and women – and children – to be offered so many hours of even the best entertainment and information; whether what we actually offer blunts their minds, deadens their passions, destroys their inner discipline. Our only criterion is success, the principle of self-preservation on the subhuman level.

How much of our armament is produced because we really think we need it for our protection; and how much is produced because we happen to have the machinery – and the shareholders – and would not know what else to do with it.?* Look at a political party or a church. As the initial fervour fades, the administration becomes more and more complex and absorbs our creative energies. It changes from an instrument for the exploration of the world and the moving of men's hearts, into a maze where we lose our way in our efforts to get to the centre – or to the top; into a tower of Babel imposing upon us the utterly arbitrary necessity of its own maintenance and elaboration. The party machine or church machine or entertainment machine requires all our attention and cannot tolerate other interests in us. It is a jealous god and visits the sins of the fathers on the children to the third and fourth generation.

The 'machine' has become our neighbour. It intrigues us, because it seems to be able – unlike our neighbour – to satisfy *all* our expectations. It imposes no limits, no shape. It permits our desires to become as vast and amorphous as the universe itself. In return, it seems to expect nothing. It is a slave that does not even long for freedom, an omnipotent slave, a god in a bottle. Why should we still look for another neighbour?

In spite of the ominous warnings of many prophets, we have

*This is no rhetorical question. The U.S.A. and British governments have subsidized the production of obsolete weapons for years.

not yet realized how subtly and profoundly the undemanding demands of the machine influence us. We are enmeshed in the vast, steely criss-cross of its unresponsive, dumb, unquestioning mechanisms which automatically establish their own time and rhythm and law. The machine does not only mould our mills and factories, but our schools and universities, our homes. It conditions our most intimate aspirations as well as our crudest ambitions. Its law, which often cuts right across the rhythm and times of our living, cannot be contradicted, it cannot be argued or reasoned away. It cannot be broken – so we fear – without breaking the machine itself. And we could not live without our slave. We have come to depend on him absolutely.

Take the instance of modern industry. Much we may boast of has been achieved. Working conditions have changed beyond recognition, real wages have increased enormously, there is an ever growing diffusion of responsibility. Yet fundamentally nothing has changed. The gods rule, only now they wear velvet gloves. The slaves remain what they were: slaves of slaves, but they are made comfortable. Even the responsibility they are offered is sham, for they are not permitted to question the self-evident axioms of the ruling mechanism. In relation to the 'machine', Western men – employers as well as employees – have no more freedom than Eastern men have in relation to the 'party machine'. They may criticize details, they must not question fundamental assumptions nor trouble about consequences. The fact that within this system of joint slavery the barrier between 'boss and men' has been lowered, that from being a tool the worker has been made into an accomplice, is of minor relevance.

Does our best hope lie in adaptation? Should we learn how to attune our lives to lifeless motions, how to throb with the strange metabolism of steel, nylon and paper, how to experience an alien rhythm as the beating of our own hearts? These are serious questions. It may well be that we are at the beginning of a completely new epoch and that our movement into it is irreversible and inevitable. Nevertheless it is important to realize what this involves. We shall be cut off increasingly from all those sources of joy and creativity which have so far been decisive in giving us the peculiar shape we recognize as human. The words of Jesus, of Plato, Aeschylus, Dante, Wordsworth, Tolstoy, will become increasingly irrelevant for us, as they register experiences we no longer share.

In the meantime, we have to admit, the 'machine' rules. In the name of its law, which is *economy*, we are already constrained to do strange things. One day they may seem no longer strange, but we, who still measure ourselves instinctively against the great words of the past, cannot yet take our strange activities and attitudes for granted.

In the name of economy[1] we allowed our industrial slums to come into existence and in the same name we hold on to them. We save on education rather than on defence, because the mechanical concept of security has already supplanted the desire for that fulness of life which might be worth defending. We save on the health services, on research into the causes and cures of cancer, poliomyelitis, bronchitis, we are willing to commit our lives into the hands of overworked doctors and nurses, because we fundamentally believe that wealth is better than health. In the name of economy we continue to devise labour-saving devices, and the time and labour thus saved we use for persuading others to buy what we have produced and to persuade ourselves that we want more, in order to save more time, in order ... And for the time left, after all the labour saving and time saving, there are other machines and other devices to fill our shrivelled minds and souls with fragmentary impressions which we are persuaded to take for wisdom, joy and life.

THE PARADOXICAL ACHIEVEMENT

It is the great paradox of our age that our dependence on the non-human tendency of 'things' seems to have increased in direct proportion to our mastery over them. As so often before, the conquerors have been assimilated by the conquered.

The scientific quest of the last few centuries represents undoubtedly a rare venture of the human mind. The reality of its achievement can still best be measured against the words of Jesus: it has enabled us, as never before, to feed the hungry, heal the sick and teach the ignorant. It has taught us to understand this world as a place made to man's measure, as a storehouse of energies and powers that can be tapped by our ingenuity in the service of life, as an order that responds to our disciplined efforts. The scientific quest has helped us to break through our dogmatic ways of thinking. It has opened our eyes and ears to new and complex experiences. Most important of all: it has compelled us to discard our lazy acquiescence in what we were content to call 'fate' – the most un-Jesus-like of concepts – by giving us the feeling of destiny, the knowledge that what we used to call 'fate' is really a challenge to be answered. It made us acknowledge that what we called 'God's will' was often our guilt.

For instance: Christians had always thought they believed that 'the earth is the Lord's'. But it was left to the scientists to show that most of our grinding poverty and its 'fateful' consequences of physical and mental decay, is man-made and not a natural necessity. Medical explorers have demonstrated how much sickness can be avoided by care, concern, the elimination of prejudices and the prevention of man-made poverty. Freud and his motley company – taking man as a 'soul' more seriously than their pious predecessors – have helped us to understand that responsibility, behaviour, character, are more delicate and complex things than was dreamed of in our moral theologies and that – for instance – crime, as the Old Testament knew, is an indictment of society rather than of the criminal it reared. Educationists have shown us that much more can be made of the 'ordinary man' than religious or irreligious hierarchies like to believe, and that invincible ignorance is often more evident in the educators than in those they are meant to lead out of darkness into light.

Yet something has gone wrong with our noble quest. Was

it the vision of their responsibility which frightened enlightened men into more mechanical inquiries, the security of narrowing specialization? Was it the old laziness of mind reaffirming itself, persuading men to accept their tentative explorations as new dogmas, to let their free adventures be turned into institutions, as dogmatic, orthodox and authoritarian as the churches they disowned? Was it our hasty pride which made us mistake our exciting discoveries on the periphery of life for the unveiling of life's enigma? Were we tempted into the scientific ivory tower by our desire for peace and comfort? Or is it greed – mammon – which makes us refuse to face the guilt our explorations have revealed, refuse to 'give and be forgiven'? Have we, in trying to keep our possessions, only succeeded in keeping our guilt? Have our efforts to protect what we have, taken on their peculiar intensity of self-righteousness, because we must try to hide from ourselves the knowledge that what we try to protect is not something 'fate' or merit has given us, but something we have taken and withheld? And do we withhold because we feel insecure and hopeless and fear that what we do not grab we shall not get? Are our economic theories much more than attempts to justify ourselves by proving that greed is natural and selfishness an inevitable response?

Whatever may be the answer to such questions, it is a fact that we have geared formerly unknown energies to our 'conservative', 'fateful' and 'idiotic' purposes and that we have become deeply implicated in an accelerating, self-feeding process over which we seem to have lost control.* We have allowed 'things' to condition ever larger areas of our life. We hand back to 'things' the responsibilities that were given to us at the time of our conquest. We have given in to the

* The platitude that our moral life has not kept pace with our scientific progress may be meant to inspire hopes of unlimited progress in the modern soul. It is a fallacy and the catch lies in the fact that moral life – the desires of man, the unpredictable, the free – is equated with 'science', the measurable, the tool. We are given the impression that morals, like a mechanism, could catch up, if only we stepped up productivity.

downward pull of matter – most of all at the moment when we discovered how to blow it sky-high. We have become fascinated by the powers we have unleashed; they have become for us the *mysterium tremendum et fascinans*, the ultimate object of our religious passion.

THE SACRAMENT OF FAITH

The shape or form man gives to that part of the world he is able to mould, is always the reflection of his deepest and sincerest beliefs. Religion is rarely the expression of our real faith and our ultimate passion. It is rather an escape from their ruthless consistency, a rationalization of their consequences, an embroidery of their offensive crudeness. Now that Marx has put his finger on it, we can no longer help seeing how much of our religion and philosophy – as well as of our economics and social sciences – is an ideological 'epiphenomenon' of the economic process, a communal self-justification. What Marx did not acknowledge sufficiently is the fact that the economic process in turn is energized by our desires, that it is the true and incontrovertible statement of what we really believe. (Our civilization, not the formula we speak in church, is our creed.) When Jesus said that faith moves mountains, he was not speaking religiously. He reminded us of a fact. At the core of man's being there is a source of energy, a passion of faith, hope and ambition, that is indeed able to move mountains. The achievements of the various civilizations that flowered in their season have left us tangible proofs. Faith is not a spiritual something, an immaterial quality, that enables us to accomplish what our minds and muscles could not. It is the life-giving –, and often life-destroying – energy behind all we do and pray for. The result of our labours and prayers is the actual situation in which we find ourselves. That situation is the palpable evidence of our impalpable faith, hope, and love.[2]

Now civilized man has always shown a marked preference for 'things'. It is at least partly true to say that up till now civilization has largely been the embodiment of man's success in 'mechanizing' man, in turning him into an abstraction, a unit, monad, number, function, something interchangeable and replaceable. Civilization can almost be defined as an order in which no one is indispensable. The army – always one of the first civilized achievements – is completely based on that assumption; so was the institution of slavery, so is the organization of modern industry and the modern search for the perfect institution or constitution. (But what distinguishes man from things is precisely his irreplaceability. The mystery of the 'I' is its uniqueness.[3])

Although the organization of our army, industry and law courts, our actual commercial and monetary policy, is never an exact and exhaustive incarnation of our faith, it is its sacrament, its outward and visible sign. It reminds us that we desire to live by the grace of the things we have made, that we want to find our security in the products of our hands, our welfare in external organization, our enrichment in the multiplication of amenities. The sacrament commemorates our barren love, our misplaced trust, our false hope. It reminds us that we are idolaters, because we believe we can find our lives in what we have made, instead of in an 'other' whom we have not made.[4]

Between me and my neighbour, the source of my renewal, stands the accumulation of the misdirected energy and passion of my own heart and mind which always want something else rather than the other, and the other only as a 'something else'. Of this our slums and our modern suburbs, our educational system and our defence policy, our over-elaborated legal and economic structures are witnesses. If their witness does not convince us, no amount of argument will – for not only the teaching of Jesus, but the teaching of everyone and everything is, in the last resort, in parables. Once again we may feel justified in thinking that our situation is unavoidable, that it is not as black as I have painted it, and that the sooner we become reconciled to it the better. It may be argued that, but for those intimations which may be no more than dislocated childish wish-dreams and romantic anachronisms, we should be perfectly happy in our accelerating comforts; that those inconclusive romantic whispers are the only dissonance in our universal harmony of complacency. And once again the words of Jesus throw their weight behind the still small voice which tells us that the seven thousand cranks who did not bow their knee to the latest fashion are on our side if we will be on theirs.[5]

THE FRIVOLOUS PROMISE

The promise of the words of Jesus strikes us, first of all, as unserious, almost trivial, certainly as irrelevant and irresponsible. It urges us who are surrounded by the gravity of things, to look – of all things! – at the birds who flit so lightly over and through everything, neither labour nor save and yet are fed, are full of life. It points at the lilies in the field who neither toil nor spin, who, in simply being what they are, achieve a beauty which even Solomon in all his glory could not match. And the promise insists that we, too, being of much more value than birds and flowers, shall live, if only we do not try so hard to keep alive. It urges us not to plan for the morrow, lest we lose today; not to look for things – as the nations do – but for the kingdom, the neighbour, and all 'things' will be given us as well.[6]

It is one of the strange qualities of life that it can be lived only today, that the day of 'salvation' is always today 'when we shall hear his voice'. We are uncomfortably reminded by the promise of Jesus that all our labours and all our planning cannot add one cubit to our span of life or to our stature;[7] that life and time and all that belongs to life and time is beyond our grasp; that when we think we can keep them, gather them into barns for future use, we are fools, worse, we are already dead.[8] The promise holds before us, as examples we understand only too well, the man who sells all he has for a thing of beauty;[9] the man who liquidates his business and home to sink his capital in a new and more promising enterprise;[10] the rascal who loved life so much that the fear of losing it taught him to cheat profitably after a lifetime of cheating to no effect.[11] The promise moves us to travel light, without change of money and clothes.[12] It maintains that it is easier for a camel to go through the eye of a needle, than for one encumbered by many possessions – mental, spiritual or physical – to enter into life.[13]

The promise calls us – and here it reaches its climax and explanation – out of the oppressive seriousness and 'responsibilities' of work and business and family building, into the frivolity, the 'irresponsible' joy of a party.[14] The most disturbing aspect of the parable of the Great Supper is the fact that the excuses offered by the invited guests are perfectly justified. Each one has something more important to do than to go to a party, and that is why he misses it – why he misses his life, 'the kingdom of heaven', for this is like a party thrown by a king made for his son's wedding.

Where the promise becomes most absurd, it becomes most explicit: it wants to get us away from our dreadfully serious preoccupations with adding cubits to our stature – or, at least, status – hours to our days; out of our spinning and weaving and gathering into barns; out of our planning and anxiety for tomorrow, into that utterly carefree togetherness of which a party is the best example. There I may meet my neighbour without ulterior motive. From there I may go out to my work – carrying dust bins or splitting atoms – if my work makes me want to return there.

Jesus insists that the challenge of my neighbour's promise is radical. Either my neighbour, or the 'machine'. Either life, or the futile efforts to feed and clothe myself. Either all things for the sake of my neighbour, or my neighbour for the sake of things. We cannot serve God and mammon. And just as we serve mammon, whom we have not seen, by submitting to the inertia of things we have seen; we can turn to our hope, which we have not seen, only by turning to our neighbour – who has become almost invisible.[15]

This brings us to one of the crucial ambiguities of the Gospel story: The words of Jesus do not seem to contain any social or political teaching, yet their central concept, 'the kingdom', was for the contemporaries of Jesus a word bursting with socio-political as well as with religious implications.

Jesus betrays no interest in the arts and techniques of government. He treats the activities of politicians as peripheral, as dishonest, as the expression and culmination of man's universal and irrelevant striving, as 'what everybody does' as a matter of course.[16] In as far as we achieve our proper human stature in striving for the things that count, 'it shall not be so among us'.[17] This attitude could be – and has been – understood as unworldliness, individualism, idealism – the words are synonyms. Theologians of all denominations have vied with the 'gentiles' to stress this point and to continue elaborating those super-personal ethics of politics and power – which were to implement what was felt to be lacking in the teaching of Jesus – under such headings as 'the two swords', 'natural law', 'the two moralities'.

Such interpretations ignore the ambiguity. They do not ask why Jesus chose to clothe his 'unpolitical' teaching in highly explosive political terms. They belittle the fact that one of the main reasons responsible for his execution was the accusation that he claimed to be a king, and that he apparently did not deny that charge, although he carefully disassociated himself from the commonly accepted ideas concerning kingship. 'My *basileia** is not of this world,' John lets Jesus say, but neither is Pilate's authority, nor that of Caiaphas. Authority is never 'of this world'. It is always based on metaphysical or suprarational assumptions. The struggle between Jesus and the authorities is not one between two worlds, but between two concepts of this world. Both are based on a final vision – of truth, right and righteousness, the adequate life – and the decision between them is an existential decision at which one cannot arrive by logical argument alone.[18]

Jesus pits his understanding of *basileia* – of authority in the city – against that of wellnigh everybody else. (Certainly that of Pilate, Caiaphas, his disciples and the great majority of christians.) We trivialize his teaching as well as his life and

---

*I use the word *basileia* here, because its connotation is wider than that of *kingdom*. *Basileia* includes the ideas of kingly realm, and sphere of influence, kingly rule, office, authority. It is centred in the man whose power creates his kingdom.

death, if we neglect to understand his *basileia* as a direct judgement over ours. The cross is supposed to have borne the inscription 'Jesus of Nazareth, the King of the Jews', that is, in the perspective of the Gospel writers, the king of the kingly and priestly nation, the king of kings. Now the point made here – and again the question whether rightly or wrongly is irrelevant – is precise: Either the authorities were justified in disencumbering themselves of a beggar who claimed an authority which they had to understand as contradicting theirs flatly; or all our ideas concerning authority in the city, the state, is put in question by the death of the beggar whose convictions concerning authority led to his execution. We have to decide between the executed and the executioner, between two irreconcilably opposed visions of the kingdom. (This is the struggle between hope and expediency; between the prophet, the poet, the educator, the revolutionist, and the statesman, law-giver, moralist and policeman. 'It is expedient', a great statesman once said, 'that one man should die for the people and that the whole nation should not be destroyed.'[19] Only he who dares to contradict in deed and in truth, is permitted to cast the first stone.)

But if our interpretation of *basileia* as of direct political consequence is admissible, how can we reconcile it with the fact that the words of Jesus shrug off all questions of practical political import as of little concern? We seem to be left with only one possible if rather startling conclusion: There is no promise for the city, the state, as such. There is only the promise to its citizens; and the most hopeful aspect of the state is the possibility of its surcease. We may hope that, to the extent we, its citizens, learn to avail ourselves of the promise, the state will become superfluous. The city is nothing apart from its citizens, and as they begin to 'realize' their responsibilities as citizens, they will leave it behind in their search for a kingdom which is the negation as well as the fulfilment of the state[20] – just as Jesus considered man to be the negator as well as the fulfiller of the law.[21] There is no 'higher good' for the state that might supersede the good of any one of its citizens. (The whole of Jerusalem had united against one beggar and his presumption. They had thrown him out of the city and had thereby, according to the words of Jesus, condemned themselves.) The city has no separate morality, since it has no separable reality. Jesus radically demythologized the Graeco-Roman concept of the polis as well as the Jews' understanding of themselves as the chosen people. (Both have nevertheless remained the christian nations' self-understanding ever since.)

Jesus stood in the succession of the prophets who – and that was their unique and disturbing contribution to history – abhorred the very possibility of a double morality. Jesus' pithy sayings gain depth and substance when they are heard together with the more elaborate protests of his forerunners. But the prophets' influence went further. What had given such power to their message was their haunting vision of the 'promised land'. The people of Israel had settled in a promised land: they had arrived; while the prophets were obsessed by the dream of a further consummation in the light of which the present stood condemned. For them the promised land had not only once been the future of the Israelites, it was their future now. They were, though in it, still far from it. And the prophets tried to persuade their fellow-men to consider the future as their promised land by reminding them of their youth or the youth of their nation when the promised land had been their future.[22] Jesus, in his parables of the kingdom which are pre-eminently of growth and movement, makes the point even more radically. The kingdom, i.e. our genuine expectation, is always in the future. Every achievement is judged by what has not yet been achieved. Everything is justified only in as far as – like a seed – it contains within itself the principle and energy of further growth. Cities with their institutions and monuments, their traditions and gravities, tend naturally towards petrification. They treat the past as their promised land. Jesus measures the city of man against the kingdom which is always beyond its grasp. He measures the pretensions of the state against the unpretentiousness of the kingdom which knows no external authority, no compulsion. (And I wonder whether Engels has not, after all, understood Jesus best, in his prophetic and repetitive insistence on the *withering away of the state*.[23] It is the glory of the state to give way to the mature man it has trained.[24] Neither Jesus nor Engels can be refuted on the ground that neither the marxist state nor the church express their aspirations.)

The words of Jesus insist that the problems of politics cannot be solved on the political level, because they are simply our personal problems writ large. And our personal problems arise from our misdirected ambitions, our fears, despairs, our love of moralism and expediency, our lack of imagination. Jesus refuses to be a judge, since judgement solves nothing.[25] He refuses to lay down the law, since laws change nothing.[26] He refuses to become an acknowledged leader, since a leader, almost by definition, renounces the attempt to influence his followers profoundly.[27] Until our personal lives are ordered and captivated by a vision that promises to fulfil all our essential cravings, the politician will have to grapple with futile and fatuous problems. Jesus does not deny that such labours are unavoidable[28] – kings as much as the poor will always be with us – but he has no advice to offer to 'kings' and little comfort. Their labours, for which they will have their reward, will not save the city from the judgement which is precisely this: the state that adores its stones, its achievements, *itself*, will be pulled down stone by stone.[29] And that will happen to every nation which does not heed the words of the prophet, the words of the man who wants to reshape it in the human image, who wants to call its children out of their stone defences to gather them – as a hen gathers her brood under her living wings.[30]

The assertion that there is no promise for the city which is not first and foremost a promise to its citizens has also the reverse implications: No promise is given to us in private or for private use.[31] What we receive and what we do, we receive and do as citizens. We cannot wash our hands – as Pilate tried to – of anything that goes on in our city. There is no longer any impersonal realm of authority or power for which we are not directly responsible. No one starves in the city, but by our consent. No one is excluded from the city, but by our connivance. We are answerable for every disorder. No one can refashion the city except us, i.e. I and you. Wherever an I and a You meet, two or three – ten or twelve at the utmost – in the name of the one who felt answerable for the whole world, there will be among them the spirit that does not find rest until the world has caught up with its future. 'Wherever two agree,' Jesus maintains, everything becomes possible. And no agreement is worthwhile, except one which wants to bring the world nearer to its future.[32] (One may think of the Gracchi, Luther and Melanchthon, Marx and Engels, Lenin and Krupskaya.)

The prophets were men who knew themselves directly answerable for and to their city. And there is no doubt that Jesus wants his listeners to be prophets.[33] By contrasting their city with its 'unrealized' potentialities, the prophets tried to make their contemporaries realize that they were living in the wrong city, the city of oppression, exploitation, poverty, complacency and futurelessness. Jesus in the Sermon on the Mount and Plain, brings their teaching to a head. He confronts all cities with their radical future. He strips them ruthlessly and gaily of all their securities.[34] He makes light of all imposed law and order, of any exclusiveness.[35] He derides capitalism in any shape or form,[36] as well as that planning which is not part of the vital and exhilarating preparation for the party to which all the poor of the world are called.[37] He holds before us a life as defenceless as that of birds and flowers, more homeless than that of foxes, as insecure as his own, as compulsively spontaneous and creative as that of trees. He makes us painfully conscious of every detail of the city – or, as he calls it, the house – we live in, by contrasting it with a ludicrously airy structure which we feel to be as uninhabitable as we cannot help finding it attractive. He ends by claiming, ingenuously and mockingly, that our city is the wrong one, the insecure one, the house built on sand and that his castle-in-the-air is built on a rock – like Homer's Troy,

Plato's Athens, Virgil's Rome and the Jerusalem of the prophets.* (cf. our *True Deceivers*, chapter four.)

*Who can deny that Jesus after his execution returned on 'clouds of power and glory' to eclipse the guardians of permanence and security who are known today only as his executioners? From a cross the presumptuous beggar has stirred the world as no king from his throne. This much he has proved: that his hope was more effective than the hopes of those who were frightened by it.

CHAPTER SEVEN

The Promise of Lawlessness

A SOCIETY becomes civilized when it has succeeded in impressing a certain coherence on the interplay of the many conflicting forces of which it is made up, when – utilizing the contradictory and complementary aspirations of its members – it has achieved poise and equilibrium, when it has imposed upon the minds as well as the instincts of its members its own definite form, idea, 'Gestalt', transcending the claims of family and tribe and gathering them into an absorbing loyalty. This intricate system of balances and counterbalances by means of which society hopes to protect itself against the dark forces from without and within, I shall here call the 'law'. It is a complicated structure, containing – often only just containing – a multitude of strains and stresses. It is a mixture rather than a compound, and its constituent parts are a strange assortment of hopes and fears, conventions and rationalizations, habits and rebellions, aggressive and defensive, protective and acquisitive instincts, conscious attitudes and deep unconscious urges. (The consciously and concretely formulated body of the 'law' is only that small part of it which – like the iceberg's tip – shows above water.) It is no accident that *justice* is the cardinal virtue of civilization. It is the most convenient and all-inclusive abstraction. It does away with all sheer humanity and does so in the most humane fashion. If, for the sake of 'law and order', we are bound to consider man as a bundle of predictable needs and computable virtues, justice is the most efficient way of dealing with him.

The 'law' protects us against ourselves, against the feared resurgence of antediluvian powers. It is *the* expression of our attempt to cope with ourselves, with our own life and the lives of others. There are many ways in which the 'law' reduces to some kind of order the thousand-and-one claims of sheer living and gives us self-confidence and the conviction that we can manipulate ourselves. Here I should like to consider three aspects of our efforts to create order out of chaos.

LAWFUL RESPONSIBILITY

We, as civilized men, feel compelled to clarify and define man's personal life. We dare not – for fear of overwhelming complexity – accept him for what he is: this most singular being, the fruit of a most singular conjunction of that man and that woman. We cannot acknowledge him as that most particular centre of the universe in which the confluence of many stars and flowers, of many faces, hands and voices becomes condensed into a most singular responsibility. We have to reduce him to manageable proportions. We have to change him, as we change ourselves, into an abstraction of rights and duties and to give a definite outline to his responsibilities. To this we expect him to conform. (And it is the comfort of conformity that it does not expect too much of him – and of us.) In return we promise to protect him against all those who may expect too much of him, as we, by turning him into an abstraction, have protected ourselves against his great expectations concerning us.

We ascribe to a man, as to ourselves, definite duties as husband, father, child, neighbour. We demand of him a certain amount of work – unless he is able to buy himself free by means of money which represents the labour of others. Above all, we ask him to be responsible for himself, to look after himself, not to become a burden, or too much of a burden, to us – in other words: to help himself. In as far as he is ready to accept himself in this role, we are willing to come to his aid when he gets into difficulties. The achievement of this abstract order is no mean feat. Within it man can find much room to become himself. He need not – and often does not – experience it solely as frustration. (I do not want to create the impression of advocating a return to barbarism.) He will often experience it as a great boon, a preserver of energies, a lubricant – like politeness – which protects him from too much friction.

LAWFUL AUTHORITY

Civilized man protects himself against the manifestation of his unruly desires by circumscribing his will to power. We create definite channels, careers, for our ambitions; checks and counter-checks for our outward-bound energies. We buttress the most haphazard institutions and conventions, legalize the most arbitrary authorities and powers, rather than expose ourselves to the free play of our passions. The instinct of survival leads civilized man to be suspicious of spontaneous leadership, of prophetic, uninstitutional, inspired authority. We have a deep fear of the disruptive tendencies of full-blooded human initiative. We like to affirm that power corrupts, because we do not like to admit that we are corrupt before we get the opportunity to exercise power. We like to ignore the fact – so amply demonstrated by history – that the canalizing of power is no cure for corruption. Civilization has not succeeded in transfiguring our aggressive instincts. It has simply turned them into other channels, different directions – competition, patriotism, ideological struggles – and made them more virulent, by giving us a good conscience, an implicit justification. It has instilled in us a fear of our emotions and instincts, as well as an undue reliance on their rationalizations – e.g. institutions, conventions, traditions.

On the other hand it is difficult to underestimate the advantages of this policy of containment. It may vitiate many noble passions, it certainly restrains many ignoble ones. It does present us with a fairly objective field of reference against which to measure our desires and ambitions. It often helps us to translate into concrete action and obedience, what would otherwise have remained a dim apprehension or a confused emotional response. It teaches us to obey as well as to command, and the more delicately responsive to its own demands civilization becomes, the more intricately will it interweave obedience and authority.

LAWFUL ASPIRATION

In the sphere of religion civilization is less original. Even the most primitive societies have their systems of taboos and observances to secure themselves against the unknown, to make themselves at home in a universe that included the invisible, incomprehensible, threatening.[1] Civilized man simply takes over the old institutions, rationalizes and refines them and gives them a new context. Fundamentally they remain the same: a protection against change, a sanctification of the status quo and the powers that be; a justification of things as they are; an attempt to give shape and substance to man's infinite longings; above all, a sanction of his human, all too human aspirations in the name of super-human powers; a desire to contain and trap in definite institutions and buildings him 'who does not dwell in houses made with hands.'[2]

It is the *strength* and *weakness* of civilization that it is always in process of delimiting the sphere of the religious: Its *weakness*, because religion is the expression – even if a mistaken one – of man's awareness of the 'other' who cannot be contained, utilized or completely understood. Its *strength*, because religion in itself is already man's effort to 'thingify', objectify that awareness of the 'other', to contain him and utilize him and to substitute for 'him' a concept that can be understood. By reducing the religious to one of many functions of communal life, civilization, ironically, frees us for the 'other', our neighbour, by enabling us to meet him spontaneously, outside the habitual pattern of family, tribe and liturgy.

Nevertheless, no civilization has yet been able to dispense with religion altogether. Whether in the shape of Christianity or Buddhism, Islam or Hinduism, Communism or Democracy, society needs the 'numinous' to keep awake in its members that loyalty which transcends their family affections and clannishness and gives them a feeling of metaphysical and moral security. Civilized religion – like conformity and authority – has its great advantages: It saves men from many idiosyncratic superstitions, canalizes his fanaticism into comparatively harmless channels – at least in as far as self-contained communities are concerned – and grants an ordered and disciplined – above all a predictable – outlet to his archetypal longings.

'LAWLESSNESS'

The 'law' is in our bones. How could we manage without it? By limiting my neighbour's demands on me, it gives me the impression that I can meet them. By conditioning me from infancy not to demand too much of him, it strengthens my conviction that I do not need him over much. It helps me to avoid seeing him as a challenge and persuades me not to become too much of a challenge to him. It protects me against the feeling of double inadequacy, against the nagging of remorse. It prescribes what it is my duty to give and enables me to keep a good conscience without actually doing to or asking of my neighbour what I should like him to do to me.

What would it involve to leave myself unprotected? The words of Jesus give the obvious answer: I have to be prepared to be beaten, robbed and defrauded.[3] I shall not be able to defend myself in the law court or on the battlefield.[4] I shall have to give to everyone who wants to borrow from me and to give in – and give doubly – to everyone who compels me.[5] I shall have to learn how to sympathize deeply with them that hate me and how to work for the enrichment of them that curse me and persecute me. In the last resort I have to be ready to die for them that would have my life.[6] In brief: my life will have to demonstrate what I should like others to demonstrate to me – had the 'law' not taught me not to expect too much.

All human law is founded on a few simple assumptions: What we happen to have, is ours. It is for me, not my neighbour, to decide what to do with it. It is better to keep what I have than to have it taken away. It is wiser to judge than to be deceived. It is more convenient to lock up the thief than not to lock up anything at all. It is better to be in control than to be at the mercy of another. Ultimately, it is better to kill than to die. It is best to do what one has to do with a good conscience.

As we all agree on those assumptions and are obviously

frightened by the alternative which Jesus, strangely enough, calls blessed,[7] one would expect us to love the 'law' for giving us comfort and pride. But we do *not*, at least not until other and livelier loves have died on us. (We cannot help feeling that the excessive lover of throne or altar, justice or liturgy, the police or the army, must be a man – or woman – who has missed something.) We fret under the 'law' and cling to it simply because we are afraid. We dislike it, partly because it persuades us that we should love to do what it forbids, and partly because we are not satisfied with what others do for us only because the 'law' enjoins it. We hold on to it, because we are terrified of what we might do if it no longer constrained the passions it rouses; and also because it permits us to withdraw, when the *other one* becomes a real challenge.

Jesus was once tested by the Pharisees, the worshippers of the 'law': 'Is it lawful for a man to divorce his wife?' (The 'law' becomes desirable where the other ceases to be so.) 'Moses allowed a man to write a certificate of divorce and to put her away.' Jesus' answer is: 'For your hardness of heart he wrote you this commandment ... from the beginning it was not so.' Here the function of the 'law' becomes clear: it is put into the place of the other, even the other that is nearest to me, my wife, because my hardened heart cannot cope with that other. I want something, at least a slip of paper, to feel justified in my refusal to admit that I have failed. 'From the beginning' it was not so, and we know it and show that we know it, by putting the 'law' between ourselves and others.[8] (Jesus refused to divorce himself from his fellow-men even after they had given him every 'lawful' reason for doing it. He accepted them and solicited them to the end and would not avail himself of what the hardness of man's heart had made expedient.)

'In the beginning it was not so.' As children – unless we were particularly unlucky in our choice – we were not aware of the authority of our parents as something external and oppressive. Our obedience – just as our occasional rebellion – was spontaneous, the free expression of a unique relationship. We were at everybody's mercy, we were not in control, others decided concerning our possessions, and yet we do not remember our childhood as a time of terror. When we begin to chafe against the authority of our parents and want to make our own decisions, we can be sure that we have left our 'beginning' behind us.

'In the beginning' a friendship is spontaneous and generous. My friend's demands on me and my imagination will be much greater than my enemy's, yet I do not experience them as compulsion. I rejoice in meeting them and him. I should not dream of putting the 'law' between us, of refusing something on the ground that it was not my duty. When, on lending my friend a sum of money, I insist on an I.O.U. – or when I begin to lend rather than give – when I begin to feel that he is asking rather much, I should admit that I have left my 'beginning' behind me.

To a young couple, the words of the ceremony that binds them 'for better, for worse, for richer for poorer' do not appear as a threat but as a promise. If they are deeply in love they will want to share their possessions as willingly as they will long to embrace. No 'law' need tell them that they ought to. Their committed togetherness will be their freedom, and if they acknowledge it, it will elicit through its frictions as much as through its harmonies those unique responses which will keep them free. A marriage that is held together by 'duty', has outgrown its 'beginning' – and its future will depend on the readiness of both partners to return to it.*

'Unless you become like little children ...' The words of Jesus not only reinforce the memories of our 'lawless' beginnings; they tease us with a possibility of return – although the return cannot be achieved by going back, but by resolutely going forward: 'After all has been done and suffered,' Jesus says to his disciples, 'I will go before you into Galilee'.⁹ Our beginnings remind us that the opposite of duty is not neglect but spontaneity; the opposite of fairness not unfairness but committal; the opposite of justice not injustice but concern and involvement. (Duty and neglect, justice and injustice, etc., are not radical alternatives. They are the two faces of indif-

---

*Most discussions on divorce are irrelevant. They are under the 'law', while marriage ceases to be marriage when it is no longer graceful.

ference – the two faces of the Janus-head which can mean war or peace indifferently.) The possibility of spontaneity, committal and concern is always present and our inability to act accordingly should not seduce us into denying it. 'Unless our righteousness is greater than that of the righteous, we shall not find our neighbour.'[10]

THE FAILURE OF THE 'LAW'

Furthermore there are our doubts as to whether the 'law' actually achieves what we claim for it. Has it ever been able to cope with 'evil', to do more than suppress certain manifestations, to canalize and moralize it? Our modern age has succeeded, up to a point, in constraining private and mob violence. Our streets are comparatively safe, lynchings comparatively rare. But while we have succeeded in establishing certain spheres of order, we seem to have become more violent and callous outside them. Race tensions are an example of canalized violence, the international situation an illustration of moralized aggressiveness. After centuries of moral theologizing, it was possible for the crusades, the inquisition, the Thirty Years War and Hitler to take place in the heart of christendom. And today we protect our 'law' – our way of life – by the hydrogen bomb.

Is it not true that the 'law', by suppressing and distorting some of our most elemental desires, has made us afraid of the very powers that are our most potent resources, and so has perverted them and turned them into something really evil? None of our psychological and physical desires is in itself evil. To desire a woman is in itself as right and good as to desire food, joy, understanding, 'salvation'. (There is a close connexion between desiring a woman and desiring 'salvation', as the Old Testament prophets knew well – and Wagner, Tolstoy and Dostoevsky. It may be that medieval theologizing became so sterile and 'law-obsessed', because it was practised by men who thought it was evil to desire a woman.) It is true that our physical promptings need an integrating discipline, as much as our intellectual and spiritual aspirations. Is the 'law' in any of its forms capable of performing this task?

The 'law' has always preached and justified the cultivation of backgarden virtues, since it is the formulation of our conviction that this is all we can hope to achieve. It has turned our energies inward and made us pedantic and conventional in private and unconcerned and apathetic in public. For our desires are outward bound, and when contained they explode in mental and nervous breakdown. Unfortunately the 'law' has also made us afraid of 'letting ourselves go'. How can we discover the true nature of our fundamental longings unless we permit them to come to the surface? Until we learn 'to let go', we shall have no chance to face up to the destructiveness that is within us, nor to make the contact with the vast energies of renewal that lie buried beneath our conventions and duties.

Although we may admit that there are many intimations and reasons which make us suspicious of our 'lawful achievements', we nevertheless cannot help feeling that the 'law' is our fate, that it is unavoidable, that it will always remain the smaller of two evils, our only refuge in a desperately imperfect world. It may be the expression of our hopelessness, faithlessness, lovelessness and timidity, the dead fruit of a barren tree; but then we are on the whole faithless and hopeless and loveless and for that very reason afraid that something even worse might befall – as if there could be anything worse than hopelessness.

THE RADICAL CHALLENGE

We must understand the significance of the three aspects of the 'law' for the whole structure of civilized life;* we must feel and know what an essential and substantial part they play in it, what real achievement they represent; we must have been hurt by the futility of our intimations and suspicions concerning them, by their majestic fatality, before we can grasp the extent to which they are challenged by the words of Jesus.

*i.e. 'lawful' responsibility, authority and religion.

Or should we rather say: until we have understood the challenge of those words as a radical onslaught on everything we take most for granted, we shall not understand the ambiguity of our achievements, their failure and their promise.

The words of Jesus call us out of the order which man has so painfully imposed upon himself. They encourage us to take lightly the claims and duties of family, clan and state; to neglect and to by-pass the roads of authority and power; to free ourselves from religion, from our longing for the objective, the proof, the metaphysical and mystical security. In the story of the temptations, which is a summing up of Jesus' work and teaching, the challenge is formulated most strikingly and radically. For the three temptations, which Jesus ascribes to the devil, are the demands of civilization, the claims of the ordered society.

Before Jesus begins his most singular work, full of a most singular and uncircumscribed promise, he feels compelled to go into the wilderness, the place which for him as for his contemporaries signified the opposite of law and order. The wilderness is demon-ridden, the home of wild beasts, the cradle and threat of every civilization: the chaos against which it tries to protect itself, the dark, unruly power it believes to have left behind. For civilized man the wilderness signifies his gravest temptation: the lure of chaos, the return of unspeakable horrors.* For Jesus in the wilderness, however, it is the demands of civilization which signify the gravest of all temptations: the lure of self-sufficiency, authority and security.

THE FIRST TEMPTATION

'If you are ... command this stone to become bread.'[11] The first temptation epitomizes the basic demand of society: 'Look after yourself, help yourself, prove yourself!' Society expects every man to do his duty, to be where it expects to find him, to prove that he can fill the place assigned to him in his own

*cf. Conrad: *Heart of Darkness.* Mann: *The Magic Mountain,* 'Snow'. Contrast the prophets. e.g. Hos. ii, 14; Jer. ii, 2; Amos v, 25.

strength. 'If you are who you claim to be,' we say to man, 'prove it to us – and to yourself – to assure us in our belief that we, too, can prove who we are. Produce what you need for your life, to justify us in believing that we, too, can produce what we need.'

Civilization idealizes and deifies work which prevents us from thinking too much of our fundamental longings and from realizing too poignantly the threat of our mortality, the fear of ultimate disappointment. It exalts the institution of the family and the concept of duty to give us security. In endues the organs of government, industry and commerce with pompous dignity in order to persuade us – and itself – that it can procure for us what we need to keep alive.

'Man shall not live by bread alone' – nor by that which exalts and mythologizes the production of bread.[12] The words of Jesus disturb us, as they contradict our superficial yet intense belief, and insist on the reality of those deeper needs and expectations we prefer to silence, because we know it does not lie within our competence to fulfil them.

Jesus, like the prophets before him and unlike many of his followers, appreciated the goodness of bread. He appreciated that man needs bread before everything else. He made the request for 'our daily bread' the centre of the only prayer he taught. Bread is the sign and symbol of his care for others,[13] of man's fellowship,[14] of the goodness of life – the 'Father's care' for men.[15] Bread is the symbol as well as the promise of man's most incredible expectation: his hope for a life which is more than the continuation of need for more bread.[16] Jesus conceded the need for work, since bread does not grow upon thorns. Yet no one was firmer than Jesus in his insistence that bread is not enough, that it is unprofitable, unless it awakens hopes for more than *itself* can give.[17]

Man wants the life bread makes possible, but even more he longs for the life bread cannot give – a life, however, he cannot have without bread. Man needs and wants the *other*, the *giver* of bread who gives more than bread, gives something of himself. More than bread, man needs somebody to trust in and to hope for. The words of Jesus explicate this longing – 'I am the bread of life; he who comes to me shall not hunger, and he who believes in me shall never thirst.' (Jesus becomes for us the *other*, whenever we become convinced of his hope for us.)

The 'law' covers up our need by persuading us that all we want of our neighbour is something – some 'thing'. We are encouraged to show goodness, kindness, love to our neighbour, but they are circumscribed by the 'law', by the very structure of our society, its ordained, ordered relationships, public and private – employer–employee, equals or unequals in the hierarchy of status or industry, even husband and wife. They all remain 'its', 'things'. We are made to feel that to give our work, gifts, talent is the highest we can offer to our fellow-men – in competitive society not even that is encouraged. Giving ourselves as Jesus understood it would inevitably disrupt the working of our society, of our clock-time system: We might miss our bus to work, because we are answering an important question – or watching a sunrise. We might lose a working week, month, year, because we want to speak to a friend, write, paint a picture, or simply meditate. Perhaps that is what the beatniks are after, a craving for the natural human rhythm, away from the organized cog-wheel, clock-time society, where we are all united under the 'law', utterly dependent on one another for our daily bread, constrained to produce and consume at the rate of the machine, the system, the 'law' that holds us together. (Everything must be deserved, not as in a home which is 'something you somehow haven't to deserve',[18] and that is why man feels insecure in the world and cannot love his neighbour freely.) The deep frustration caused by our loss of independence instils a grudge towards our neighbour and kills our sympathy – turns him into the 'Neighbour' of Kafka.[19]

Jesus breaks through the 'law'. He refuses to give or to promise anything which is not himself: 'The bread I give ... is my self. I myself am food.' In the concreteness of his words, in the definiteness of the image he has impressed on the men that heard him – or hear him – Jesus hopes to become what we really want of our bread.*

Jesus' hope brought him into open conflict with the 'law'. He did not work, for he believed that he had more to give than what his hands could produce. He refused to understand his responsibility as society wants us to understand it. He neglected its demands for the fulfilment of definite duties. He would not be bound by its will to assign to every man his well defined sphere. He became a vagrant and a beggar. Unlike the 'foxes that have holes and the birds that have nests, he had nowhere to lay his head'. He declined to produce what modern society demands before it even concedes us the right to work: a permanent address.† He insisted on meeting his fellow-men in all the nakedness of his humanity, simply as the son of man, a man. He wanted nothing to re-enforce his claim, no irrelevant semblance of authority, no respectability. He demanded the same attitude of his disciples. He called them out of their occupations – fishing for bread – because he had something better to do for them – fishing for men.

He sent them out like sheep among wolves, without arms, without references, without money or even a change of clothing. He calls them out of their family commitments – he who does not hate father and mother, wife and child, cannot be his disciple – and two of them leave their father in his boat with his nets and his servants. He does not acknowledge his own mother and brothers, when they come to him. Those who hear his words and take him for what he is, are his brothers and sisters and mother[20] – and there is of course no reason why his family should not become, what they had always thought they were, by listening to him as if they heard him for the first time. For the family as an institution is of no account. Only

* Note carefully the whole argument of John vi. The bread awakens the hope of the people. But it is only something that 'rots', like the manna in the desert – and those who ate it. The true bread is the self – the 'flesh' – of man – 'the son of man' – our very definite and singular neighbour, his words, his spirit.

† What I want to say here is not weakened by the fact that vagrancy was then neither as rare nor as much frowned upon as it is today. Luke ix, 58 makes this clear.

what we actually become to one another by continually involving ourselves in one another, turns legal fictions and physical facts into human realities.

Jesus makes himself our neighbour and our brother – as against all the requirements of the 'law' – by the power of his promise. 'Man shall not live on bread only, but on every word God utters,' on every word our neighbour speaks to us as if he were our God. Jesus offers more than a man can give and insists that it is precisely that 'more' which man desires and must learn to ask for and to offer.[21] Jesus cannot vindicate his promise. He simply lives – and dies – as if he could become for us what he promises. For him the promise is perfectly real. He wants us to accept it and become such a promise in turn. This promise inspires us, since it lays bare the character of our desires: in its light we come to understand ourselves and feel ourselves understood.

Two Gospel accounts may serve as illustration. 1. The *Woman of Samaria* whom Jesus meets at Jacob's Well, at the place of an old tradition, did not know that she was looking for 'living water', 'the well springing up unto eternal life'. Unwittingly she had been looking for it five times under the 'law', for she had had five husbands. Now she has sought it in defiance of the 'law', only to discover that the one whom she now has is not a husband. Jesus becomes for her what she was seeking. He makes her understand her desire by acknowledging it as her true self. He becomes her prophet by promising what man cannot give and what, nevertheless, we want of man and can find only through man – the son of man.[22]

2. When Nathanael hears about Jesus, he is not impressed. There is nothing apart from Jesus himself that could impress. 'Can anything good come out of Nazareth?' When Jesus tells him; 'I saw you, when you were under the fig tree,' Nathanael recognizes him for the fulfilment of his expectations. 'Sitting under the fig tree' signified to the Israelites a waiting for things yet to come, for the 'Messiah', the kingdom. Jesus takes Nathanael's expectations seriously and becomes for him the one he has been waiting for.[23]

Our acknowledgement of Jesus as our neighbour – or rather

to acknowledge Jesus' estimate of our neighbour as the most hopeful one – is as simple and as difficult as the response of Nathanael and the Samaritan woman. Nothing will convince us, until the words of Jesus discover us and compel us to take ourselves as seriously in our expectations as *they* do. And this will always mean at best non-conformity, if not rebellion. For a man to take himself seriously in his great hope – to become himself, to be a friend and to importune others for friendship – hardly fits into a society whose raison d'être is to guarantee our daily bread – making hope, as in the prayer of Jesus, unnecessary. And the guarantee costs us no more than our dream, hope and vision.[24] As with advancing age these grow ever more illusory, we are easily persuaded that the price we pay for our bread – for belonging to an ordered society with its duties and corresponding expectations – is after all negligible.

THE SECOND TEMPTATION

'The devil showed Jesus all the kingdoms of the world in a moment of time. To you I will give all this authority and their glory, for it has been delivered to me and I give it to whom I will.' In this second temptation the 'devil' becomes transparent. We need not accept him as a mythological figure, although, undoubtedly, he was so understood by many, perhaps by Jesus himself. The 'devil' is simply that which makes us believe we can shape our own destiny and which would persuade us that external authority is the one guarantee of 'law and order'. That is to say that man can be governed, contained and changed only by some kind of force, that we are justified in the existing state of affairs. The 'devil' is that which simply wants to be acknowledged as the way of the world – and all things will be added unto us. 'If you then will worship me, it shall be all yours.'[25]

In resisting this promise as a temptation, Jesus not only rejects the cruder aspects of power – the methods of obvious coercion, oppression and exploitation – but the use of all those subtle expressions of authority which man dons to convince himself that he is important, that his position confers on him an authority apart from that inherent in his words and actions. Jesus will not be a king whose word has to be obeyed, a priest whose action is holy, a judge whose sentence is law. He refuses to go the way of self-justification: to exercise an authority which is that of an office and not of a person. He does not even become a rabbi, a qualified teacher, to give weight to his teaching – he refuses 'office', because he wants to remain untrammelled in the service of his hope: 'him only shall you serve'.

Jesus does not rebel against authority – in that respect alone he is not a revolutionary. He knows that rebellion takes authority too seriously. Unlike the revolutionist who never hopes for more than the perpetuation of authority in a new form, Jesus' subversive influence is directed against all forms of authority. 'My kingship is not of this world; if it were, my servants would fight.' He neglects authority, by-passes it, treats it as irrelevant for the more serious business of living. For him it is that which has to be left behind. 'It shall not be so among us.' We are to persuade, not to coerce. His words remind us that the way of authority and the way of hope are incompatible. 'I have come to bear witness to the truth. Everyone who is of the truth hears me.'[26]

The words of Jesus help us to understand our understanding: When do things become meaningful and true to me? I have to be of the truth before I can hear it. I have to have understood before I can understand. That is why truth that matters, existential truth, is always revelation, unveiling. It can do no more than show what is already there. That is why Jesus is primarily a witness. Any position of authority would only hamper his witness, would tend to turn it into a generalization, legalization would destroy it. The question remains: what hope is there for man to be changed, to become righteous, to see the truth? The 'law' has no confidence in man's transfiguration. Hence its attempts subtly and crudely to compel him for his own good. Jesus simply witnesses and only those that 'hear' will follow. What about those who are not 'of the truth'? – Predestination? Fate? – Is not the 'law' more humane and merciful? It does not demand so much. It simply asks man to conform to a given righteousness, rather than letting him risk finding his own truth, Yes, the words of Jesus are hard. But is it not this hardness man fundamentally craves for: the test he secretly wishes he could meet and become at last a man in his own sight – more of a man than one who climbed Mount Everest, a man who will no longer have to *prove* to be stronger, more clever and more righteous than his neighbour?

Jesus insisted to the end on remaining true to his vision, his witness. He succeeded in raising the whole machinery of law and order – of the 'devil' – against himself. He thereby revealed – to them that understand! – the nature of 'law and order': it is our refusal to recognize 'God' in our neighbour, to see him as greater than we permit ourselves to be. He demonstrates that the 'law' can only kill the neighbour whose hope importunes us beyond endurance.[27] (He also shows us that there has been at least one man who preferred remaining true to his vision to a life under the 'law'.)

THE THIRD TEMPTATION

Jesus experiences man's desire for the miraculous, for religious certainty and metaphysical security, as the final and subtlest temptation. Twice he has answered the insinuations of the 'devil' by 'religious' quotations, by asserting his reliance on something which seems to stand over against the claims of all human achievement: 1. Man does not live by that alone which he has made. 2. He needs an authority which captivates him. Now the 'devil' regains the initiative. He himself becomes religious. He quotes texts from the Bible. 'He will give his angels charge over you, to guard you' and 'on their hands they will bear you up.' He bids Jesus put his faith to the test, to experiment with it, to find out whether his reliance was justified. We do scant justice to the devilishness of the 'devil', if we mistake his final onslaught for a simple abuse or distortion of holy wisdom. The temptation would have been harmless and Jesus' rejection of it insignificant, if it could have been reduced to a question of correct interpretation. The 'devil' knows his Bible better than many theologians. He puts his finger on precisely those passages which epitomize the very contentions which Jesus has so far put forward to defend himself. To do so – *c'est son métier* – makes him the 'devil'.*[28]

Let me try to paraphrase: 'You have decided to live by hope rather than by fact, in the power of the possible rather than in that of the actual, by that which is signified rather than by that which is.† You have made this decision because you believe your hope will be vindicated against the facts – *all things are possible to him who believes* – your desire against the pressure of the actual – *mountains can be moved by faith*. You believe your craving for purpose will be vindicated against the persistent purposelessness of all things – *the son of man ... rejected ... killed ... will rise after three days*. You have decided to ignore the way of the world in favour of a movement which is the way of failure. *I, when I have been rejected, will draw all men to myself*. You have put your trust in something that cannot be proved, cannot be known except as an intimation. You are determined to stake all on your obedience to a power that seems to you to defy all the powers that be. Now then, if you think you are right, put your faith to the test; see whether you really believe; whether whatever you claim to believe is real, whether you are not staking everything on an illusion.'

In rejecting this insinuation as a temptation, Jesus rejects religion. He turns his back on man's archetypal attempts to delimit the miraculous, to secure himself in his beliefs, to put his aspirations to the test of 'reality', to give concrete shape and context to something which, by its very nature, can only be experienced as giving *us* shape and purpose.[29] Jesus did not turn away from man's great expectations in order to turn towards smaller ones. He did not consider religion as a temptation because it requires faith, but because it does *not* require faith – because it turns faith into credulity.

Religion is man's – especially civilized man's – most astonishing *tour-de-force*, his most paradoxical achievement, his most glorious Pyrrhic victory. It represents his recurring,

*cf. *The Brothers Karamazov*, Book 11, ch. 9.

†Hoskyns and Davies: *The Fourth Gospel*, pp. 284–6.

almost successful attempts to twist the apprehensions of his inadequacy into a more or less self-contained and self-explanatory system. It traps his intimations in a set of doctrines, translates his aspirations into dogmas and creeds, his infinite longings for a final encounter into assumptions and self-evident truths.* It substitutes for the unknown and unknowable – which challenges and invigorates us – the 'known' or 'revealed', the 'soon-to-be-known', the only too well known.[30] On the other hand, having 'explained' the real mystery, religion creates mysteries where there are none, enables us to withdraw from the mysterious insecurity of life into pseudo-mysteriousness.

We are always tempted to turn our provisional insights into a religion, because we hate above everything else insecurity.† Religion gives us the feeling of ultimate security, offers us something definite to believe in, persuades us that we know what we believe and convinces us that we really believe what we think we believe. There is therefore no need for us to pay attention to Jesus and his elusive promise, to the unverifiable claims of a neighbour and the inconsistent promptings and longings of our own heart.[31] We may now believe in a creed, a scientific theory, a political manifesto – or in the uselessness and nothingness of everything. Religion also gives us the opportunity to experience the 'joy of fellowship' of shared beliefs and convictions on comparatively inexpensive terms. We are saved the trouble of finding out in intimate personal encounters whether there is anything to be shared. We need not become 'martyrs', stake our life on our beliefs, since there is at our back an institution to vouch for us. Religion justifies us in all we do – *c'est son métier* – for even when it admonishes us in our failures, it does so by letting us know what we should have done. It justifies us in our defence of the *status quo*, in our rebellion against it and in our withdrawal. Religion is the apotheosis of the 'law'.[32]

* e.g. the 'doctrines' of the Trinity, redemption, ontological and un-ontological proofs of God's existence.

† That is what makes religions of ideologies. Communism, Capitalism, Agnosticism can be religions.

The more sensitive and imaginative a man, the greater his vision and hope, the more fiercely will he be attacked by doubts and the nightmare of meaninglessness and chaos. At times, an unbearable insecurity threatens the order and rhythm of his life, his very sanity. To go on living at all he must be sustained by an absolute purpose and final meaning. Hence the third temptation was also Jesus' greatest. It is to misunderstand him, if we take his belief in 'God the Father' for his final security. His rejection of the 'devil's' offer proves this. Jesus stands without external crutches, a man who does not tempt providence, does not call on superior authority, takes responsibility for what he does and is.[33] 'I am.' Blasphemy? Certainly in the eyes of all of us who dare not take full responsibility for our lives, our desires and visions, who are overwhelmed by the fear of failure and final meaninglessness. It is the fearlessness in face of possible illusion[34] – a greater courage than that which faces death – which fascinates and frightens us in Jesus, if we take him seriously.

The guardians of mankind, the lovers of men, who have pity on our weakness and failings, rightly condemned Jesus as arrogant and blasphemous, as an enemy of the people. Jesus wastes no time on 'com-passion', *Mitleid*.[35] Like the Old Testament prophets he is too full of the burning vision of the great potentialities of the life before us – the kingdom. He confronts our weakness with audacious and presumptuous confidence in the possibilities of living, with an almost frivolous disregard for the safeguards of the 'law' concerning the great spiritual values that contain and often wonderfully sublimate the great longings of the human heart.[36]

Hence Jesus' rude attack on pharisaism for which we have to read today 'religion'. According to him religion is our final hypocrisy, because it compels us to pretend that we have finally arrived. It rejects the commandment of life, which is the commandment to grow into no-one-knows-what. It makes us shut the kingdom – which is growth – in men's faces and keeps us from entering ourselves. It honours the dead prophet because it is afraid to listen to the living voice. It turns spontaneity into duty, grace into a burden. It makes life stale, turns it into painted death and rounds on him who wants to wake the dead.[37]

Who is Jesus that he dares attack the highest authority representing man's most civilized achievement? How dare he rob man of his greatest gift, his spiritual security, 'God', replacing it by a mere promise of a life not yet realized? And here we come to Jesus' most shocking contention for which he paid with his life: namely that he and the 'Father' are one.*

Jesus lived for his hope. He did not treat it as something he could adapt to the demands of 'reality'. He subjected 'reality' as well as himself, to it. He obeyed it. He let his whole life be a witness to it. His hope was his God.[38] In as far as he lived his hope and would let nothing come between himself and his hope, he had the right to say: I and my hope are one. He who has seen me has seen my hope.[39] (None of us can say this, for none of us has the courage to accept his hope as his God. Ultimately our god is fear or resignation. We are never one with our hope.) Jesus was one with his hope, and therefore completely responsible, as we never are. 'He who has seen me, has seen God': The miraculous working, the moving of mountains, is no longer left to providence, to 'God', but becomes the power of the son of man, of Jesus, of man.[40] From now on we pray for the poor by feeding them, for the sick by healing them and for peace by disarmament. The responsibility cannot be passed on. Into the place of the 'God' who answered questions we had already answered, who revealed what we had always known, steps Jesus, God become man, and raises questions we dare not ask – hopes we dare not dream of.[41] (He calls *us* into hopes which make us restlessly responsible.)

Jesus called his hope 'God', 'Father', 'Lord'. This would have come natural to him. The words were vibrant with vast, concrete, hopeful association. They would have stirred the imagination of his hearers as they no longer stir ours. They

---

*It is, of course, the greatest achievement of religion to have succeeded in making man's most violent attack on it into its main support. I believe that Nietzsche is right in thinking that in christianity we are face to face with man's supreme priestly achievement.

would have given the kind of substance to their imagination they could no longer give to ours. I do not want to say that there is no 'God' – a statement as meaningless as to say 'there is' – I simply want to insist that, like all the sayings and teaching of Jesus, his words concerning the 'Father' are parabolical. That is to say, they are intimations of something to be grasped and understood only within the very movement of life, and to be discovered only 'on the way' together with the one who speaks these words. If we seek to discover the reality of these sayings in any other way we shall be faced by a riddle without a solution, worse: by a word without meaning, the word 'God'. (No 'heavenly meaning' will make matters any clearer. It will rather obscure the living 'earthly meaning'.)

We can say that Jesus trusted in his hope, had faith in it, as long as we remember that we are using mythological or poetic language. Especially when talking about *faith* we must guard against formulae, against trapping the living thing in abstractions.[42] Faith, Jesus' faith, is nothing in itself, nothing we can see or hold even for a moment. That is why it often seems no more than an illusion, most deceptive and most fascinating.[43] Life becomes petrified – often very imposingly so – joyless, stagnant, because we want to perpetuate and immortalize the moment. But, paradoxically, the lasting things are the fleeting moments, the sudden glimpse, the unexpected inspiration. To catch them without killing them is hard and requires all that passion, that 'faith', of which the great artists and poets have given proof. All we can say – because it is all we know – is that faith, like love, is a movement, an activity of the whole person – most truly a passion. It is a passionate going out with my great hope towards what it promises, towards what moves me, heart, mind and body, to go, to follow into life and more life – into a kingdom.[44]

We also know – but often like to forget – that this 'faith', this going out with and towards my hope, is lost, as life is lost, at the point of death, when humanly speaking – and how can we speak otherwise – all is lost. At that desperate and terrifying moment, Jesus, our neighbour, gives us no direct comfort. There is nothing in Jesus, not even his 'faith', that overcomes the cross. He is nailed to it heart, mind and body. His activity, his 'movement into life', is at an end – he loses faith. We hear the words: 'My God, my God, why have you forsaken me?'* He has lived his life, in his great hope, uncompromisingly to the end. His hope can go no further than the end. There is no call of defiance, no triumphant shout of the human hero – or the christian martyr. Neither is there a mystical, last moment revelation of something indestructible in man – the 'soul'. Jesus dies, in spite of his great hope and faith. And perhaps it was because he hoped so much and lived so intensely that it was so hard for him to die and christians through the ages have, after all, been justified in calling his death the most terrible of all.

Yet we are faced with the fact that Jesus is understood to have gone into his hopeless death in hope. It is recorded that he believed that the energizing power of his life would not come to an end with his death; that, on the contrary, death would give to his life a new and surprising fruitfulness. It would make it altogether more hopeful, in as far as it demonstrated that there is the kind of life and hope for the sake of which a man – passionately in love with life – was willing to pay with his life. Jesus believed – so the words of Jesus want to make us believe – that death accepted as the culmination of such a life would round it and make it complete.[45]

And it is a fact that the life of Jesus has become – in spite of or because of his death – a parable of hope.[46] And if we consider anything in the world for more than a parable, we are idolaters. And if we consider anything for less, we lack – for better or worse – the faith that took Jesus to a cross.

To sum up the Three Temptations: We dare not put reality to the test of hope. This was precisely what Jesus did to the bitter end, to the point where – as far as any 'hopeless' or 'faithless' view is concerned – reality had finally contradicted his hope and him. And yet this is the point of encounter: a cross, two sticks of wood, which either signify nothing, in the sense that nothing matters or what matters is *nothing*; or they

*Like many critics, I believe the other words from the cross to be theologizing additions.

signify a hope and faith which *nothing* can negate, which survives its own death.

Jesus pitted himself against the 'law' and all its claims and that is why, according to the 'law' he had to die. But there is a 'law' according to which we all have to die. That 'law' – like the other 'laws' – we accept. Jesus did not. (cf. *True Deceivers*, chapter five.)

CHAPTER EIGHT

Forgiveness

I HAVE tried to show in what sense we have to understand not only the teaching of Jesus but also his life and death as parabolical. The whole event we know as 'Jesus of Nazareth' – and ultimately we cannot distinguish between Jesus and the words of and about Jesus – is a parable. It has retained such hold over Western man's imagination precisely because it has resisted all attempts to turn it into anything less ambiguous – e.g. into dogma or myth or a moral tale. It is above all a parable of 'lawlessness' – of the hope that the 'law' is neither the last nor the best answer to life's real quest – of *forgiveness*. For the antithesis of the 'law' is not licentiousness, which is no more than a recoil from the 'law', but forgiveness. In this chapter I want to show why I believe this parable to be relevant for us, why our life – and today quite literally the life of mankind – may depend on a proper appreciation of its implications, and why an existential understanding of it may well be our only hope of escape from the logic of the 'law' threatening to sweep us into totalitarianism – whether political, commercial or cultural – total anti-totalitarianism, total war, total annihilation.

FORGIVENESS IN THE OLD TESTAMENT

According to the Old Testament which, as far as we know, was the only book Jesus knew well, forgiveness belongs to Yahweh alone. For the Old Testament writers this was not a doctrinal statement. It was the explication of their own experience that man cannot forgive. Yahweh *forgives* by calling man into a purpose, a hope beyond that by which he had been content to live. He lures him away from his humanly limited aspirations into an adventure which nothing except the reality of the achievement can justify. He liberates a crowd of slaves, takes them out of a bondage they had learned to take so much for granted that even the desire to break free had become atrophied. He entices them to rebel, against hopeless odds, by reminding them of the imaginary youth of their tribe, of their frustrated youthful desires. He seduces them by vast promises to go where they would never have dared to go. He coaxes them to listen to the commandments that will make men out of slaves and will help them to feel at home in a greater order and harmony.* He inspires them to take a land they would not have conquered on their own initiative. *That is his forgiveness*.

Those great historico-legendary events are understood by all the Old Testament writers as the beginning of Yahweh's forgiveness. His further mercies – 'and they endure for ever' – are seen as a continual recalling of his people into their beginning. When the prophets call the Israelites into renewed obedience, trust and hope, they point to the archetypal pattern of Yahweh's work: The people of Yahweh are encouraged to hope in him, because he was and is the awakener of their hopes: to trust in him, because he has vindicated his trustworthiness; to obey, since their obedience, unless freely given to their liberator, their hope, will be claimed by the powers of oppression from which he wants to set them free. Yahweh's forgiveness is his persistent calling and recalling into hope, trust and love. It is his refusal to take 'no' for an answer, it is his importunate wooing. He jealously insists that the people of his choice† do the impossible: rely on a strength beyond their own, a possibility without precedent.

(e.g. Isaiah warns the people against any political alliance. Yahweh, not the strength of their horses, will defend Jerusalem. Jeremiah urges the Israelites to hand their country over to the Babylonians in the hope of a 'return', a 'resurrection' they cannot expect if they cling to their forfeited city. See also

---

*The *commandment* is the challenge from 'beyond', from the realm which confers authority. (See p. 86.) It is the call into an order man can never quite reach. The 'law' is the perversion of this transcendental challenge into an immanent achievement, an available possibility.

† Hope cannot be chosen, it chooses whom it wills. 'I have mercy on whom I will have mercy.'

the exilic prophecies of Ezechiel and especially of Deutero-Isaiah. Finally Zechariah: 'Jerusalem shall be inhabited as villages without walls ... For I will be to her a wall of fire round about, says the Lord, and I will be the glory within her.' All these prophecies want to be understood as realistic assessments of the political situation. They contradicted the 'realism' of the contemporary kings and statesmen which history proved to have been unreal.)

Yahweh insists that his people take him seriously, not only as a ruler, but also as a husband, a lover. He insists on becoming for them that 'other' – the invisible, always to be rediscovered 'other' – who can give them what no one else can, who heals their diseases, who inspires awe because he forgives.[1]

Jesus accepts and sharpens the Old Testament view. He understands forgiveness exclusively as an opportunity grasped,[2] a call answered,[3] a responsibility shouldered,[4] as a giving of what one expects.[5] Forgiveness is altogether an activity. That is why they who do not forgive are not forgiven, and why only those who experience the world as a standing offer of vast opportunities cannot help desiring to give more to their fellows than they are able to.[2] Forgiveness is of the future.[6] It has nothing to do with forgetting or wiping out the past; for the past is unchangeable, hopeless, dead – to be buried by the dead. And deadness, everything that was already dead in the past – the refusal to live hopefully, to appreciate one's gifts and opportunities – is unforgivable. The man who buries his talent will die,[4] while the rascal who uses his wits to cheat himself into life will live.[7] The man who misses the chance of giving others a chance,[2] because he did not appreciate the chance he had been given, has missed his chance. He who refuses to obey his inspiration, his hope, can *never* be forgiven.[8] Or, in other words: as long as we refuse to live hopefully and inspired, we shall not live. Forgiveness becomes real and effective when the dead are stirred by a new voice,[9] when new energy is poured into us, when life looks promising once more, when the impulse to give and be given, the conviction of 'being sent',[10] becomes obsessive, when the future looks like a promised land to be taken by storm.[11]

FORGIVENESS OR DEATH

Neither in the Old nor in the New Testament is forgiveness understood moralistically. We do not experience our moral shortcomings as our real failure in life. The great and small decisions everyone has to make, the habits we acquire, the attitudes we feel compelled to assume in our profession, marriage, friendship, often reveal themselves – when it is too late to undo the damage – as consequences of cowardice, faithlessness, hopelessness etc. They are rarely the consequences of consciously evil designs. (Few of us are big enough to be consciously evil, to do something we cannot justify before ourselves and others.) The evil of which we are aware presents no great danger. It is forgiven the moment I recognize it as evil – not, of course, as 'the smaller of two evils'.

Of the real corruption at work within us we are not aware, though we may see it clearly in the other, the enemy, the rival, who, more often than not, sees it clearly in us. We are not aware of it, because it is the corrosion of the very desires, passions and longings which the 'law' has driven underground. This corruption is at work not primarily in our shortcomings, our 'sins', but in our efforts to justify ourselves in our modest virtues. Moralism is its subtlest camouflage, for it keeps us preoccupied with a few symptoms while the rot spreads. It is this corruption which needs to be 'forgiven'.

The New Testament understands sin as unbelief – not as immorality – as our inability to believe in our opportunities. We are sinners, not because we do this or leave that undone, but because we refuse to follow our hope, to trust our desires, to obey our vision; because we prefer to unlive our lives and cannot help fearing that to live them involves too much of a risk; because we feel secure only in doing that which denies the possibility of growth.[12]

(On the other hand, the New Testament treats sin as something that has been overcome, left behind, that can be and has been forgiven; that can be understood for what it really is only in the experience of forgiveness – as something past. For sin is the refusal to take my chance, to grasp my opportunity. And until I have grasped it I cannot know what I should have missed if I had not done so.[13])

Our failure to live up to our aspirations can, of course, always be construed as 'realism'. We are wiser now than we were in the beginning. We have learned that our hopes were foolish, our desires romantic or idealistic – and we shall have to learn how to justify our failures and explain them as fate, 'being only human', 'no saints'. Now the words of Jesus want to persuade us – and that is their forgiveness! – to acknowledge our failures not as fate but as guilt. He urges us to admit that we are responsible for what we are. He furthermore tries to make us see that such an acknowledgement, far from being depressing, is a most joyful and liberating experience: for sin can be forgiven, fate can not; and sin is forgiven the moment we experience and acknowledge it as a foolish – not a fateful – betrayal of a better opportunity; the moment it is revealed as a burden, a desire for what is undesirable; the moment we begin to long for that which our guilt has betrayed.[14] The words of Jesus, by holding before us a fulness of experience we had long since despaired of, make it tempting for us to turn our aspirations once again towards the never-quite-attainable – which is their true object – away from that which is not worth attaining.[15] When the words of Jesus compel us to acknowledge our failure as guilt, we have realized their power of forgiveness – and all sins can be forgiven, except self-righteousness and complacency which deny the need for forgiveness.[16]

Forgiveness cannot condone evil, since it is intrinsically that which reveals evil as evil. It is the energy that saves us from decay, the courage that bids us laugh at fear, the passion that breaks our apathy, the hope that overcomes despair, the love that saves us from indifference. It is the action which lets the other find sympathy where he expected vindictiveness, concern where he expected hatred, generosity where he expected retribution, which gives much because it expects much, which recreates new opportunities for the other, because it apprehends the world as a vast bundle of opportunities.[17]

The Healing of the Paralytic[18] – the 'miracle' – is one illustration of Jesus' understanding of forgiveness. A man comes to him full of great expectations. (His pallet has been let down through the broken-up roof.) He has already turned away from his past and towards the unexpected, his neighbour. Jesus therefore states: 'Your sins are forgiven.' To explicate his meaning he adds: 'Rise, take up your pallet and go home.' Forgiveness is a particular and singular encounter which restores a man, enables him to pick up the threads of his life again, puts him into a new context, turns his desires into actuality, asks him and empowers him to make use of the very faculties that have become atrophied, compels him once again to become a full member of the human community. Forgiveness is that event in our life which forces us out of our private world into the society of our neighbours of whom we had despaired, into tasks we had come to consider beyond our strength. It is an 'eschatological' event.[19] It faces us with the promise of our *beginning* and the hope of our *end*. It questions us searchingly: 'Do you want to do again what once you thought you could do? Do you want to take up what you thought you were able to carry? Do you want to turn to your beginning, an older and a wiser man? Do you want those visions, you dreamed of when you were young, restored? Would you like to hope once more that you are moving towards an end which is a new beginning? Do you want to follow your hope to where nothing is as yet certain and everything is possible, rather than remain where you are, where there are many certainties and few possibilities? If you do, then take up your bed and walk! Believe that you can carry what for so long has carried you! Go to the others from whom your debility, your faithlessness and hopelessness had separated you and *walk* among them, dance and jump,[20] that you may become for them a symbol of hope!'

All the Gospel accounts of healing can be understood as parables of forgiveness: the world is given back to a man, a man is sent back into the world: The blind see, the deaf hear, the dead are raised up; a hand is unwithered, a back unbent and feet made nimble. And each time it is an event not explicable by the laws of cause and effect – by the rule of averages – a result not to be obtained by the 'works of the law'.[21]

'WITH MEN IT IS IMPOSSIBLE'

I am painfully conscious of being unable to forgive in that fashion.[22] At best I can refrain from condemning others in the hope that they will not condemn me. I can behave as if they had not offended me, hoping they will behave towards me in a similar manner. But I cannot forgive my neighbour his inability to become for me what I most desire, namely my 'saviour', my hope. Nor can I expect him to forgive me my failure to become this for him. We cannot – and this is our dilemma – create for the other the situation in which he could realize his full stature, become truly himself and thereby truly our neighbour. (See *Distant Strains of Triumph*, Beatrice.)

We find a moving example of man's intrinsic inability to forgive in the Old Testament story of David and Absalom. When David hears of the death of his rebellious, beloved son he cries: 'O my son Absalom, my son, my son Absalom! Would I had died instead of you, O Absalom, my son, my son!' Yet even if he had died for him, died at his hand, would he have resolved the chaos created by the rebellion of his favourite son? He had not been able, in his life, to become for him the other that compels love. Would his death have redeemed the situation? Would it have made of Absalom the king he wanted to be and the Israelites needed? Yet the truth of the matter is that David declared his readiness to die after the need for it had disappeared. Was he insincere? More than any other man? There had been the moment when he had almost decided to stay in Jerusalem, to face his victorious son. But the realistic counsel of his courtiers had prevailed. Had he been wise or faithless? Forgiveness is always unprecedented. It creates a unique situation and we shall never know the outcome, unless we have taken the risk.[23]

Forgiveness is not at our disposal, because we are involved in each other's failures. We are implicated in every crime in every act of faithlessness, hopelessness and apathy. We shall never know whether any particular outrage was not a direct result of our lack of faith, hope and love.[24] Every criminal is an indictment of the society that has not been able to 'save' him. There is no 'innocent' party to a divorce, just as there is no innocent party to a war, only two groups of people who have failed to become promising to each other and have decided to shelve the fundamental issues by escaping into the irrelevancies of the 'law' and of violence. There is no accused who is not also an accuser, no offender who has not first been 'offended'.

The belief that forgiveness is at our disposal is a misunderstanding and leads to hypocrisy. It is corrupting to behave as if one had forgiven, when one has not. My enemy leaves me more dignity than he who treats me to that kind of pardon. Everything Nietzsche has to say about the 'forgiving and compassionate' is true. Furthermore, such forgiveness is based on an unbearable and unjustifiable arrogance: Who am I to forgive, to degrade my fellow-man by treating him as one who needs me more than I need him? Such forgiveness is the expression of a twofold hopelessness: We have ceased to hope *for* our neighbour, we accept him at his lowest and thus betray him more effectively than our hatred could. We have ceased to hope *in* him, to expect from him the deed that might forgive us, become for us the challenge that will change us. We have destroyed him as a brother. We have become tolerant, which is the highest refinement of self-righteousness and invincible ignorance, and have made ourselves intolerable to the one who wants anything rather than our tolerance.[25]

Unless we recognize the biblical understanding of forgiveness as a flat contradiction of our own, we shall be neither particularly startled nor encouraged by the unexpectedness and originality of Jesus' words and actions. He is not only shown as continually doing the unprecedented, but as insisting that it is the only thing worth doing. Jesus speaks and acts as if man could forgive, as if it was, if not the easiest, at least the most natural thing to do.[26] The Pharisees were deeply shocked when they heard Jesus say: 'Your sins are forgiven.' They thought they knew that 'only God can forgive'[27] or, as we might put it today: forgiveness is possible only if there is a 'God'. They realized – what two thousand years of pious preaching has made hard for us to realize – that Jesus' action implied a most extravagant claim, namely that from now on man is 'God' when he forgives.[28] On the other hand, Jesus never says: 'I forgive.' Such a statement would be meaningless. He says: 'Take up your bed and walk.' He forgives or, rather, makes us realize the possibility of forgiveness, by confronting us with situations which make the temptation to start anew almost irresistible.

Nothing except the utterly unprecedented, the sudden vision, the poignant encounter, the intuition that there is, after all, something teasingly hopeful and promising about my neighbour,[29] the intimation that he might – perhaps simply by accepting my help – become my 'saviour',[30] can forgive me, give me back to myself. Nothing except exuberance can 'send' me,[31] as Jesus felt himself sent, and sent his disciples – to the end of the world – to face all nations with the hope of the unprecedented – warning them that where their hope was not proclaimed there would be no hope.[32]

The words of Jesus are not satisfied with depicting *him* as having done the unprecedented, but want to seduce us into repeating what, in spite of all precedents, can never be anything else but unprecedented action. His command to forgive is no moralistic exhortation. It does not ask us to do this or that, but to stake everything on a reaching out beyond our strength and to expect a beginning from beyond our end.[33] It asks us to do what can only be done in hope, in a by-passing of the 'law' with its securities and assured rewards.[34]

If I want to live rather than die, forgiveness is a necessity. Quite simply: if I am not willing to reach out for the impossible, I shall not get it. I shall die, for death is the ultimate precedent, the one possibility under the 'law'. The forgiveness of the words of Jesus consists in the fact that they continue to pester me by presenting the impracticable as practical, the unrealistic as real, the inopportune as my great opportunity.[35]

THE FIRST SUPPER

Death is not only the ultimate precedent 'under the law', it is also the end of my responsibility, the point where, at last, I am released from the 'law', its restraints and burdens.* The coward in me is freed from fear, the fighter finally unmanned. I am given certain peace at the cost of uncertain victory, rest at the price of possible transfiguration – i.e. of a possible forgiveness, of a possible 'other chance'.[36]

Jesus, after a life of 'lawlessness' and unreserved responsiveness, takes complete responsibility for his death. He does not go to it for peace and rest, but to measure his hope against it – in search of a new possibility and consummation.[37] He 'dares' death, invites it to become responsive to his hope. He compels death to speak for him, to yield significance, to fulfil his life and hope. Can his failure, his death, really become a new opportunity? Can it be forgiven? Jesus does not even ask that question. He is so much one with his hope that he simply affirms that it can, that his death will be forgiven.[38]

His disciples sit before him and argue over the kingdom, plan to defend it, quarrel about rank and honour – all Judases betraying their actual hope. They, too, expect of their neighbour, even of Jesus, a thing, a kingdom of crowns and thrones. They do not realize that they have already got their kingdom, that it is already among them, sitting at their table, sharing a meal with them. The kingdom has come, they are in it, and they do not know it. They cannot acknowledge the free, spontaneous communion between man and man as their ultimate destiny. Their ambitions – like ours – bypass their friend, the 'son of man', man. (They seem to have no great need of him. They turn his life into waste. They kill him as

---

*Even where the 'law' tries to tighten its hold over men by projecting itself beyond life in the shape of heaven and hell, it demonstrates its irresponsibility. Heaven and hell are completely irresponsible, they are fixed, they require no fundamentally new response.

they have killed millions of sons of men in the course of history.)

In face of this complete blindness, incomprehension and uninspiredness of his friends – men he had taught and loved most intensely – in defiance of their failure and unforgiveness, against all laws of probability, Jesus remains true to his hope for them, his friends, who betray him – his enemies. He goes on taking them seriously in their great expectations, affirming that what his life could not, his death would do: give them another chance to reach out for the true kingdom, as they will come to realize its worth in their loss. He believes that they will yet return from their misdirected ambitions to *him*, that they will want *him*. ('Peter, do you love *me*?') He takes bread and breaks it: 'This will happen to my body. It is broken *by* you. It is also broken *for* your sake.' He pours out wine: 'This will happen to my life. It is wasted because of you. It is also "poured out" for you. Let the act which reveals your betrayal of your friend become for you the reminder of the opportunity you missed. Let it recall you into the fellowship you made light of, into the fulfilment you shrugged off so easily. Whenever you come together to eat and drink, let that which nourishes you and that which gives you joy remind you of your destiny which will always be that fellowship you rejected when you rejected me, your friend and neighbour, your hope.'[39]

Those words make of Jesus' Last Supper our first. They transfigure the end of his life into a new beginning. By those words he makes himself responsible beyond his death and beckons us, again and again, to return – with him – to our first meeting with our great expectation: 'I shall go before you into Galilee.'

THE CROSS

What we cannot forgive Jesus is not that he broke the 'law' – men strong enough to do this have always had our secret if not overt admiration – but that he did not give us a new one. We can forgive Barabbas, literally give him another chance, for he does not basically challenge our 'lawful' assumptions, but simply replaces – even if violently and treacherously – one order by another. Jesus gives us no 'law'. He gives himself. We are shocked, frightened, dismayed. We do not know what to do with a man.[40]

If at all we put ourselves into the hands of another man, he must be *trustworthy*. We certainly cannot trust a man without power; and the only power we recognize as effective is the 'law', though it be the 'law' of terror. (To the power of love we pay lipservice: we reserve for it a limited field within the 'law' and so make it powerless.) We certainly will not trust a man who cannot prove himself to be equal to the 'law', and the one sure proof a man can give us, are his works and his defence and justification of those works – his 'righteousness'. They are the sign of his trustworthiness, his being true to his word. Yet fundamentally we do not trust any man to be true to his sign – we do not even trust ourselves – though we do, of course, acquiesce temporarily and accept provisionally – always under the protection of the 'law' – his official trustworthiness. Jesus does not even give a sign and is therefore, by definition, utterly untrustworthy.[41]

But we have to have something to put our trust in, something that will preserve our trust by not putting it to the test too crudely, something other than man – bigger, safer. The 'law' as religion – ever our helper and preserver – supplies us with this 'God', someone who would save us from ourselves, live for us, and, above all, promise to salvage at least some of our great expectations, dreams and visions which here and now we have to sell to 'reality', to death – the final end of our secret hopes for forgiveness, for another chance. So we are allowed to cheat 'reality' – cheat safely, without risking our hope – on condition that we do it within the limits of the 'law', that our last, final chance be and remain safely and indefinitely postponed – a situation which, though hopeless, offers the understandable peace and rest that come with the final exclusion of the unforeseen, the unexpected, unprecedented. In short, the 'law' offers someone who will live for us and beyond us, since we dare not stretch beyond our rationed, apportioned, death-bound means, dare not live beyond ourselves.[42]

But the words of Jesus want *us* to live and to live beyond our means: forgiveness, the final chance, is here and now.[43] Again I am shocked and frightened. First it was the undefined, unproved complexity of a sheer man that got between me and my often painfully formed and acquired image and order of existence. Now it is the immediacy and urgency with which I am confronted by the visions and hopes I thought I had given up to the 'devil' long ago, often at no small cost. The more of a man I am, the more soundly I shall have tested my hopes and the better shall I have recognized their true possibilities, their limitations. The Pharisees, Caiaphas, Pilate – the grand and small inquisitors and philanthropists – the temporarily trusted masters of men, all have tested their great hopes, justified and established them; they have turned what they could of them into reality – they have paid their admission fee. And now they live to defend that reality. What more do we want and expect.[44]

Again we cannot forgive Jesus, this time for belittling our hard-won achievements.[45] We cannot forgive his insistence that we did not do what we really wanted and expected to do. As if we did not know it! As if it had not cost us dearly! – The more sensitive I am, the greater my expectation 'in the beginning', the more I shall find Jesus' importunity intolerable. And yet what great hopes he resuscitates in me, what unsuspected fulness of life he makes me recognize in myself![46] I am almost willing to give everything to follow that voice. But why will he not prove himself, give me some sign? Why will he not stand up for his own truth? Why is he on the cross he could so easily have avoided?*

This I cannot forgive Jesus. It is his worst offence, for it touches my deepest hopes concerning man: He has failed to be my hope and saviour, for how can I be expected to hope that he can save me, if he cannot save himself? 'Come down

* A theology which teaches that the cross 'had to be' has already avoided it.

from the cross'* may be a vulgar taunt, but then vulgarity is the bitter fruit of men who feel themselves cheated of their glory.[47] Jesus himself had set fire to the great expectations of the people. Someone would come and do away with the powers that be – which they mistook for the Roman occupation. He had taught them to hope for everything to be made new, had stirred in them the mad hope for complete forgiveness.[48] He let them call him king, Messiah, Son of God. – And then at the cross, everything remains as before. Nothing has changed. – I cannot forgive Jesus this failure: his death, that has robbed me of a hope I never dared own before Jesus' words had nurtured it; the hope that I will not fall if I step outside the 'law'; that my outcast state – being derided, persecuted or simply ignored – and my very failure to stand up to it or even to risk it, will not make me a failure, because I shall have another chance.[49]

And now at the cross, all is as before, nothing has changed. I have no reason to take my hope and great expectations seriously, for the one who did, and so led me to take them seriously, is dead. I shall, after all, not be forgiven, as Jesus was not forgiven. He suffered and died for his failure. – In my better moments I wish it could all have been undone, all have been otherwise. But I bow to the inevitable and accept even this hopelessness, his death, which he had done nothing to avoid.†

Yet the words of this man Jesus give me another chance; and if I will not take it – they say and I know it to be self-evident – there really is going to be no other. 'Forgive and you will be forgiven.' If I want another chance, I shall have to give the man Jesus another chance – as Barabbas had been given another chance. It is useless to call: 'Come down from

*When we smile humanistically that, of course, that he could not have done, we are less human than the Pharisees. When we smile piously that only 'God' could do that, *our* 'God'; that, as a matter of fact, he has done it, had left Jesus on the cross only to perform an even greater miracle, we have understood less than the Pharisees.

†I do the same when I turn the certainty of his death into a certainty of life hereafter, for I thereby turn forgiveness into a new 'law' – a new hopelessness concerning this life.

the cross and we will believe.' We shall have to take him down ourselves.*

But are these not mere words? After all, we did *not* forgive Jesus; we *did* nail him to a cross; we did *not* take him down. We failed. We killed him. And the 'law' teaches, quite rightly, that there are actions which, in very fact, cannot be forgiven, that it is too late, that we have missed our chance.

So Jesus' expectations concerning us remain unfulfilled? And here again, where we should like, above all, a clear and certain answer, all is ambiguous: We are 'only' given hope – or is that after all the other chance, the chance always promised by Jesus: 'Forgive and you will be forgiven'?[50]

Quite simply: to those who believe that man has failed – if we believe that we have finally failed – that there are points of no return, Jesus is dead. To those who share Jesus' great expectations concerning man – expect much of themselves and of others – who go on reaching beyond themselves, Jesus lives.†[51]

The cross is the symbol that even failure to forgive can be forgiven – at the price of forgiving. It is possible for a man – Jesus – to take me seriously in my 'infinite longings', even when I have failed when I have to all intents and purposes, betrayed them and him who fathered them.[52] He trusts me, though I have not given proof of trustworthiness, have revealed myself as untrustworthy, have proved irresponsive and irresponsible. He gives me responsibility, makes me, once again, and in spite of all, responsible. And there is no greater responsibility than to forgive, to give to myself and to others the chance to prove ourselves in our great expectations – to

---

*Had the Pharisees really wanted him to be their 'king', they would have had to take him down from the cross. Had they wanted him to be their 'God', they would have had to become his. This is the uncomfortable insistence of the cross and of Jesus: What we do to the least of his brethren we do to our neighbour who is our life and our 'God'.

†Did the great expectations of the disciples revive because they knew Jesus lived, or did and does Jesus live because their hopes had revived? To those who 'live', this question smacks of the problem concerning the egg and the hen.

trust that we shall do great things, if we really hope and want to.

THE RESURRECTION

Resurrection is the 'incarnation' of hope, the 'realization'[53] that there is always hope: that no damage is irreparable, no failure final;[54] that only the dead need bury the dead;[55] that life must not be looked for among the dead.[56] Resurrection is the movement towards the hopefulness and faithfulness of Jesus[57] whose hope and faith in us and our neighbours was – so we hope – justified.[58] Resurrection occurs in our witness to him[59] who, to the end, witnessed to a hope that was greater than he,[60] that inspired, transfigured and uplifted him, and will – so he hoped – continue to uplift, transfigure and inspire us.

The Resurrection is not a separable event.* Even the New Testament itself does not allow it to add one inch to Jesus' stature. It is the implicit promise behind the crucifixion, the aspect of the cross which has made it impossible for the Western world to escape from its insinuations. It is the formulation of the hope we dare not hope and without which we dare not live.[61] It is the terror at the prospect of an empty tomb – the final intensification of 'those obstinate questionings ... Blank misgivings of a creature/Moving about in worlds not realized.'[62] It is the revelation – which comes to us as we ponder the hopelessness of man's sufferings – that tragedy is a necessity, since only hope that triumphs over necessity can inspire hope.[63] It is the expectation of a repetition of the unrepeatable,[64] the promise of a 'return', an incredible 'always' and 'everywhere'.[65] It is the challenge to *live* our lives, to let our life become a source of life to others, to realize that others cannot have what we withhold. The Resurrection is the

---

*To treat the Resurrection as an *historical event* is to misunderstand the meaning both of history and Resurrection. History is concerned with the past, the fixed, the dead. Resurrection is concerned exclusively with the future, the moving, the living. And again: to treat the Resurrection as an historical event is to make of it the sign Jesus refused to give, because it would absolve us from looking for *significance* in this world. The Resurrection, on the contrary, is the formulation of Jesus' insistence that either everything or nothing on this earth is significant.

challenge to take this life and this earth seriously, because everything is a parable, a beginning and not an end in itself. (cf. *True Deceivers*, pp. 214–27, 232–45.)

Postscripts to Chapter 7

IDEOLOGY

OUR aspirations are the purposive aspect of our imagination. They are growing points and therefore changeable by definition. As we develop – perhaps by reason of our faithfulness to our aspirations – they are bound to become modified, transfigured. Now the more our ideals mean to us, the stronger the urge to pass them on to others and to eternalize them. Here lies the danger of all teaching and communication: that in the eagerness and earnestness – I am taking man at his best – to impress the good news on my brother, I shall be tempted subtly in two ways. 1. I shall be disposed to turn *my* insight into *our* insight – and so destroy it. For my understanding which has taken years to unfold – years of searching, faith, failures, betrayals – my singular, peculiar insight, cannot be turned into formulae which other equally singular and peculiar beings can understand and accept directly. Is then our noblest attempt: 'to make others hear our voice', doomed to failure? This fear and doubt makes me all the more impatient to shout across the abyss. I must be heard at all cost. I cannot wait for the slow maturing. My brother may be lost, unless I save him quickly. He may reject me before he has understood and all will be lost. So I search for the magic formula, generalize, simplify, dogmatize. I turn the life-giving word into a 'law' and betray my brother and myself. 2. I shall tend to turn my insight into an 'eternal' truth, as a justification of my life and a monument to its worth.

The temptation to take these shortcuts will remain powerful in our modern age. The means of communication have increased enormously, while the gulf between the 'cultured' and the 'uncultured' is as wide as ever. In spite of universal education, the power of articulation is still all on one side, and the inarticulateness of the others is taken for simplicity or worse. Intellectual arrogance has got into our bones. We, the articulate, – though we may protest to the contrary – cannot help feeling that we have to condescend when speaking to those who cannot meet us on our level of argument. (And since the many have been given 'equality' they have to be addressed.) Specialization has made matters worse. In many fields we all are inarticulate, in one or two we are experts, addressing the mass of the inarticulate. This explains the universal tendency to popularize and banalize when speaking to the outsider, to use jargon, become precious and esoteric when speaking to initiates. This tendency can be seen at work among scholars, scientists, politicians, artists and theologians. It corrupts hearers and speakers. It turns ideals into ideologies, aspirations into vested interest, theories into creeds, convictions into idolatries – the growing points of life into dead ends. Such a perversion is tragic and very dangerous. The energy that was to burst into growth will, now that there is no possibility of growth left, become explosive.

We become guilty of ideological fossilization as soon as we begin to think in terms of 'We' and 'They' (see page 141), turn others into the 'enemy' (see page 146), are willing, for our idea, not only to die but to kill (see page 143).

Ideology traps us in uncritical self-righteousness. Having made the division into 'We' and 'They', we shall always find excuses, justifications, at least extenuations, for *our* actions, words and motives; hidden intentions, evil motives, duplicity or sheer wickedness in *theirs*. The ideological sleight of hand consists in the exploitation of the fact that every human action is ambiguous. This gives to much of our propaganda – implicit and explicit – the semblance of reasonableness, and so makes it more dangerous than a lie. Half of what I say about my enemy may very well be true – just as half of what he says about me is probably only too true. (We might begin to shake off our ideological captivity by listening carefully to what our 'enemy' says about us and by consistently imputing to him the motives we quite naturally attribute to ourselves.)

Ideological self-righteousness is based on a further misunderstanding and dread. It believes that goodness needs to be defended, since it is much weaker than 'evil', that 'evil' must at times be called upon to defend goodness – especially that particular kind of 'evil': 'the smaller of two evils', without which, so we are convinced, no goodness can survive. Ideological habits make us forget that goodness is a concrete and particular response to a given and most concrete situation. It is simply that which, under any circumstances, makes for more and a fuller life. Goodness is incomparable, cannot be measured against another good. My good is not yours. What is good for and of England may be bad for and of China. 'Judge not and you shall not be judged' is not a moral precept, but an exhortation to refrain from doing the unprofitable. We can only judge ourselves – even that no more than provisionally – for there is no situation except our own which we can understand existentially.

Jesus who had so much to communicate is perhaps a bad advertisement for un-ideological teaching. He did not dogmatize, etc., nor did he try to clarify and explain. He spoke in parables, in riddles. He, too, wanted to be heard, but he knew that only he 'who is of the truth would hear his voice'. Those 'outside will hear and not understand'. Was he callous to believe that it is better for a man to remain deaf than to misunderstand; better not to be saved than to be saved the trouble of discovering his own truth? – Everything is said and done in parables, Jesus told his disciples. And when, near the end, they say to him: 'Now you do no longer speak in parables, now we understand clearly', he answers: 'Now you will be scattered.' – According to Jesus there is no final understanding which is not a misunderstanding.

'WE' AND 'THEY'

The scientific and technological revolutions, though they have implicated us in their inhuman tendencies, have also impressed upon us the fact of our human togetherness. They have enabled us to see what, in former ages, not even the bubonic plague had made us see. We are now compelled to acknowledge as a fact what until recently was no more than a pious phrase: the brotherhood of men. We are together 'for better for worse, for richer for poorer, till death us do part'.

Unfortunately we have not yet begun to assess the implications of this fact, still less have we succeeded in making it the basis of our instinctive response – though, if it be true that instincts are the instruments of survival, this is precisely what should be happening. Two world wars have demonstrated our togetherness. A third may prove it beyond contradiction – leaving none to contradict. We have experienced a recession that started in New York, produced chaos and misery in England and Japan and contributed not a little to the rise of Hitler and almost managed to destroy the order – or disorder – that produced him. The thoughts of a Jewish prophet brooding, in the British Museum, over the wickednesses in high places, are now agitating Chinese peasants – and us through them – because they did not, at the time, agitate us enough.

We know all this, but the knowledge is not yet in our marrowbone. It cuts across too many prejudices, mental and emotional reflexes, vested interests. Even in the face of annihilation, the obliterator of all distinctions, we cannot help clinging to the most arbitrary one of the 'we' and 'they'. How can we acquire, before it is too late, the instinctive habit of always and radically thinking in terms of 'we'?

(The little words 'we' and 'they' are, of course, a most convenient grammatical device. In that sense I shall continue to use them freely. But I want to insist that they are no more than that. They correspond to no reality – metaphysical, ontological or epistemological. At any moment, when they refer to human beings, they are interchangeable. The 'we' can become 'they' and vice versa. They can be subsumed under the one word 'we' at any moment and under any circumstances.)

For instance: The problem of overpopulation is not 'theirs' but 'ours'. We all shall suffer, unless we take decisive, intelligent and imaginative action at once. In the same way, economic problems are always 'ours'. To think in terms of 'looking after ourselves' before we have time for 'them', is not only wrong but idiotic in the strict sense of that term. There are only we ourselves to be looked after and that will always mean first and foremost, to look after those of us who are in greatest need. Once we have learned to think in terms of 'we' only, we can no longer say: 'First our country, then . . .' because our country is an organic member of 'our' world. We may still store grain in our silos while others are starving – like the wise man of the Gospel story – for hearts are not easily changed by new thoughts. But we shall not find it so easy to justify such action, for the verbal sleight of hand has been taken from us. We are withholding something from ourselves, in order to have more than we have. We are starving ourselves in order to save up for a rainy day. And our defence policy? We are spending vast sums of money to defend ourselves against ourselves. Nothing is more necessary – for we are indeed dangerous – no method more futile. In helping the poor we help ourselves, we protect ourselves against our own hunger and fear of hunger. We can no longer say 'we disagree with the Russians, we distrust them'. We can only say 'we and the Russians cannot agree, we distrust each other and ourselves'. We may no longer say or think 'we are right, they are wrong', but 'we hope we are partly right, we know we are partly wrong'.

We have lost the excuse: 'we cannot do this or that, until they do it'. For until 'we' do it, it will not be done! For instance: 'We cannot disarm until they disarm.' Such a statement is based on a double fallacy. a. The fallacy of mistaking grammar for metaphysics. b. The psychological fallacy which lies in the failure to recognize that 'they' in 'their' minds have always been 'we', that 'we' in 'their' minds have always been 'they', and that therefore nothing can be done until 'we' do it. My contention is, of course, not just a logical *tour de force*, but another way of interpreting the words of Jesus: 'follow me'. 'Peter said to Jesus, "Lord, what about this man?" Jesus said, " . . . what is this to you? Follow me!"'

FREEDOM

Easily troubled by the singular and unclassifiable difficulties that arise whenever we take our fellow men seriously, we like to take refuge in abstractions and generalizations such as justice, equality, freedom. They create for us a deceptive appearance of order and peace. They present a clear cut challenge – unlike my neighbour – and call for reactions rather than response. I should like to consider two abstract concepts, by way of example: 'Freedom' and the 'Enemy'. The first is an essential ingredient of all present Western ideologies – except for such atavisms as fascism. The second is present in all ideologies. We can even go further and say that its presence betrays any system of beliefs as an ideology. The 'enemy' is the symptom of ideology. He is the ideological disease *par excellence*.

Liberty as it is understood today in Western political thought and propaganda is the late flowering of a long historical process, the fruit – almost the hot-house fruit – of a combination of favourable circumstances, not primarily an achievement. It has taken shape and substance from many contradictory aspirations and required many years before it imposed itself upon the strivings of our factional interests and persuaded us of its desirability. Such liberty is not so much threatened by an 'enemy' from outside, but by our own twofold misunderstanding of its nature. 1. In thinking of liberty we make the 'category mistake': we treat it as a thing, a something extra that can be abstracted from the complex and subtle interplay of the many forces and institutions of our modern society. 2. We mistake liberty for the whole of freedom, we forget that it is only a small and not necessarily essential part of it. It is the smile of the cat, not the cat.

1. Liberty is an aspect of that peculiar balance of forces and interests which becomes possible when a community is no longer violently divided over any fundamental issues. It presupposes a fairly high standard of living, a reasonably fair distribution of wealth, a long experience of political independence, a high degree of centralization, thorough literacy, a civil service tradition. Unlike freedom, liberty is largely a matter of institutions, associations, conventions. Now all such structures have a strong tendency to ossify, to perpetuate themselves and stifle the very thing they are to express. For liberty – like freedom – is changeable and alive. It feels as constrained in yesterday's fashions as a Bikini girl in Victorian bathing

costumes. When we no longer wish to incarnate liberty in new forms, we can be certain that it is ailing. At this stage a certain decadence, a readiness to think of compromise more highly than of pursuing an issue to its conclusion, a habit of trusting in committees more than in prophets, becomes obvious; And the question whether liberty bought at such a price is still worth having is being raised – not always by the best of us.

It is at this stage that we begin to talk about 'liberty having to be defended' – which it cannot. It must be lived and remains alive only as long as it is outward looking, missionary and aggressive – not necessarily in the martial sense. Walls destroy liberty, though they be built with the best intentions. Liberty shrivels when it fails to see the 'enemy' as part of 'us', as those of us in greatest need of persuasion. For especially the 'enemy' – whether within or without – can only be persuaded by the beauty and usefulness of liberty itself.

Liberty cannot be preserved. What our fathers fought for and accomplished was very different from the mere consequences they were able to hand on to us. Every generation has to recapture and re-achieve its liberty. Nevertheless, the fact that our fathers have prepared the soil and given us a pattern is not to be despised, and we have to remember this when we turn to other countries who lack the conditions of natural growth. We cannot expect them to become liberal democrats, until the economic conditions are propitious and some definite political and social traditions have been established. Until then we should not condemn them for not enjoying liberty, if we really believe that liberty is something to be enjoyed. (By the way: We are not afraid of communism, because we believe it will take away our liberty, but because we have lost our belief in it. Our apathy, the corrosion of our aesthetic, moral and intellectual appreciation by the indiscriminate use of mass media is a more dangerous enemy than our 'enemies'.)

2. Freedom is infinitely more than liberty. It includes the thousand-and-one responses we are free to make towards our neighbour. It may include liberty, it may develop it. It can survive without liberty, while liberty can survive freedom as little as the smile the cat.

It is a great freedom to be alive, as all those who have been near death know well. It is a great freedom to love, to marry and bring up children, to develop one's body, learn to use tools and play instruments, pass through joys and troubles, come to know men and women, pictures and symphonies, etc., etc., etc. In a society where people still fall in love, found families, become artists, craftsmen, scientists, doctors, ballerinas, actors, conductors, inventors and so on, people are not unfree however much they may lack the gracefulness of liberty. Those many skills of heart, mind and body are the preconditions of liberty and a society is free – even if not yet 'liberal' – in as far as it fosters and encourages them. (On the other hand, the most democratic constitution cannot compensate for the actual lack of freedom among people whose creative powers are sapped – are democratically permitted to be sapped – through hunger or surfeit, insistence on competition, mechanized entertainment, sexual overtittilation, etc.)

To speak, for example, of nuclear warfare as a possible defence of liberty, to imply that it is better to die and to kill indiscriminately than to become slaves of our 'enemies', is not only callous but foolish: we are ready to kill the cat to save the smile! The fact that we can think in terms of nuclear warfare, proves that we have fundamentally no love for liberty – let alone freedom – for any nuclear conflict will involve not only us and our enemies and those that neither love nor hate us. It will destroy the freedom – not only the liberty – of future generations, who will be born deformed and mentally deficient, unable to exercise the freedom of deciding whether or not they would have been willing to endure their fate for the sake of our liberty.

THE ENEMY

This concept is our most fatal abstraction, since it seems to point insistently to a most concrete being, namely the one who has or might hurt me. He is nevertheless an abstraction. No man as such is my enemy. At best I have abstracted and made absolute a limited and particular aspect of his life: his 'having anything against me'. Usually he is merely the product of my personal or communal fears, the projection screen of my inhibited desires, the result of conscious or unconscious propaganda.

Jesus does not deny the existence of the enemy, he does not try to argue us out of our belief that there is such a one. He simply asks us to deny him existence *as* an enemy. We are to see him as just another man we are free to love. He may be the very neighbour we need – the 'good Samaritan' – because he complements us, because he seems so different from us. He is the man who, more than any other, challenges our humanity, discovers us, makes us see what we really are – 'sinners who love those who love them'. He is the man I most readily condemn and in whom, therefore, I am most clearly condemned, 'for the measure you give will be the measure you get back'. By judging him I am judged, for by acknowledging him as my enemy I compel him to acknowledge me as his and to see me as I insist on seeing him.

In my enemy I see myself. In him I could – if I would – see myself as my greatest enemy. By loving him I could – if I would – learn to hope again and to love myself. Through him I could learn to love the man and hate that within me which makes of him an abstract thing.

I fear my enemy, because he wants what I have. I hate him because he has what I want. (He is always in possession of the 'promised land'. The Old Testament tells us that we cannot enter that land until the enemy has been annihilated. The New Testament adds that we can enter that land only by annihilating our enemy as an enemy. Our arch-enemy is Jesus who in his attempt to destroy our enmities united all enemies against himself – Pharisees and sinners, Romans and Zealots, Sadducees and scribes – for how can we continue to live self-respecting lives without enemies? Yet Jesus claimed to be in possession of the kingdom – the promised land – which we shall not be able to enter until he has become our friend, that is until our enemy – the least of his brothers – has become our friend.)

My enemy is mean, since he will not trust me; presumptuous, since he expects me to trust him. He refuses perversely to see life as I see it, and I suspect he waits for the opportunity to compel me to see it his way. My enemy is my safety valve: in him I can freely condemn what I uneasily feel I should condemn in myself. He is, so it seems, necessary for my life. I need him more than a friend, for if he did not exist, I should have to face up to the disorder that is within *me*, I should have to destroy *myself*.

It is another aspect of the Passion Story that Jesus, by refusing to become our enemy, compelled us to create him as one. He turned the other cheek, did not resist evil, asked that we should be forgiven, and thereby demonstrated that the 'evil' is in us who cannot bear to be faced by one who refuses to be an enemy. In what Jesus lets us do with him, he reveals that the enemy is always of our own making. He is man-made in the image of man.

My enemy ceases to be my enemy once I see him as the 'other' who is not made in my image – nor by me – whose concreteness consists in his otherness, who is my 'you'. The 'you' is always concrete and repeats, in a multitude of shapes, the same challenge and promise. My enemy wants to be known as my 'you', wants to be understood imaginatively, sympathetically. He wants to be invaded, filled by me, and in turn would penetrate and conquer me. He needs to be loved most of all when he seems to hate me; for only love can convince him of the futility of his hatred.

Of course, there is much evil in my enemy, as there is much in me. He is full of greed, narrowness, selfishness and prejudices, just as I am. I have good reason to be afraid of him, since I have good reason to be afraid of myself. And precisely because of this, the words of Jesus urge me to love him. I love myself in all my greed, self-centredness, ignorance. I love myself even when I see much in myself to be ashamed of. Even when I think I hate myself, I only hate what I feel prevents me from becoming myself. 'I was not myself', I say. – I must have a vision of my enemy, as someone who also wants to be himself and cannot.

As I am afraid of him, hate him, distrust him, envy him, I would – at least in my better moments – like him to make the gesture to convince me that the fearful emotions he awakens in me are unjustified. This therefore is exactly what I am bound to do for him, if I wish to become the kind of person I wish him to be, that is, a neighbour and not an enemy. In the last resort, when everything else has failed and my fear and hatred would persuade me to think of murder and hydrogen bombs, the only thing I can do is to die for him, for there is no other way of proving 'to the end' that I take him seriously as a person, a 'you', that I will not take him seriously in his perversion, in his mistake concerning me, his enmity.

Everything I have said about 'my enemy' acquires a new intensity when he becomes 'our enemy'. Here the abstraction becomes complete and its concrete consequences become terrifying. I do not really know my personal enemy – else he would be no enemy – but I am at least acquainted with him. We are not even acquainted with '*our* enemies'. Our fear of them is sheer dread, Angst, a pathological response to the unknown. As our dread of the unknown which presents itself in such threatening form becomes intensified, our inhibitions become weakened. Defending ourselves against an abstraction in defence of another abstraction – liberty or justice – we are ready to do away with 'them' as well as with ourselves, demonstrating beyond doubt that we hate ourselves in our enemies. In spite of my fear and hatred of 'my enemy', I should find it difficult to kill him with a good conscience, as our common humanity will force itself upon me. Yet we do not seem to be troubled by the killing of many of 'our enemies', for they remain an abstraction for us even in the killing. This is especially true of modern warfare and makes of it the demonic thing it is.

Footnote: We have often tried to defend our preference for abstractions in the light of a further abstraction: justice. And justice is also an excellent term to justify us in the consequences of our abstracting: the just war.

FORGIVENESS is primarily imagination in action, the 'growing-point' of life-in-togetherness. It is the feeler, the antennae, that reaches out into unchartered space, the tendril of the climbing plant that gropes for and curls round everything that promises support for further growth. It is the opening of the blossom for fertilization, of the eye for the whole world to fall in, of the ear to the infinite variety of crude and subtle harmonies. It is a tasting, smelling, sampling, a hungering and thirsting for ever more complex experiences of communion. It is also a wooing, courting, importuning, a never-ending creative endeavour to bring into existence new conditions and situations for an intenser and profounder exploration of our common human heritage.

Unlike easy indigence, forgiveness is not an escape mechanism. It does not idealize the other, nor the self. On the contrary, it gives us new insight into formerly unsuspected depths of failure, neglect, helplessness and pettiness, in others as well as in ourselves. The hopefulness of imaginative forgiveness is a practical, realistic, unsentimental attitude: We have heard a miraculous promise. We know ourselves bound up with others who may or may not have heard. We begin to hope that the promise can be 'realized'.

To forgive is to witness to my vision of neighbourliness, to give concrete expression to my hope that I might yet be able to give what I continue to expect, to hunger and thirst after a righteousness I have not yet achieved. Forgiveness reveals my poverty as well as the validity of the promise that is given to those who know they are poor. I am forgiven and able to forgive when I am obsessed by the desirability of the scarcely feasible, when I long to give, because I am greedy of the 'good measure, pressed down, shaken together and running over' which, in return, will be poured into my lap.

In the following notes I want to glance – arbitrarily and

very briefly – at a few of the problems that arise from our refusal to grasp the opportunities offered.

I. FORGIVENESS AND MARRIAGE

No marriage lives up to its expectations – least of all when the partners claim it does. No marriage is a full utilization of all the possibilities it offers. Somewhere even the luckiest of us fall short. We sell our birthright for a mess of pottage.

We relinquish the adventure for the sake of security. We get tired of the life-giving friction which restores warmth and sensitivity to any human relationship, and hold ourselves apart for the sake of 'peace'. We cease from exploring the other, either because we find the quest too strenuous, or because we suffer from the delusion that we have discovered all there is to know. We are content that the first intensity has vanished, that our passion is spent rather than transfigured. We become satisfied with one another – which is only another form of being satisfied with oneself. We lose the unique experience of a deepening personal communion by frittering away our vital energies elsewhere and separately, or we allow our intimacies to become barren by concentrating too exclusively on one another. We tend to mistake the acquisition of furniture for the building up of a home. We betray our aspirations for our children's sake – 'we must give them a good education' – and thus betray our children. Or we neglect them and one another, because we have ambitions. Etc., etc.

Forgiveness in marriage is a passionate turning and returning, time and again, to the beginning of our love, hope and zeal. It is our unreserved acknowledgement of failure and our active longing to have it redeemed. It is the re-affirmation of our first hope that life, the wholeness of it, is yet before us. It is a resolute turning away from everything that is a compromise with death, a compromise on account of the belief that sooner or later all will end. We forgive one another in marriage, when we refuse to be satisfied with one another and with ourselves, when we keep moving, hoping that we are on the way towards our real beginning, that even our first one was only a parable, a foretaste of the final consummation that is always before us. We forgive, when we are ready to have our heart broken rather than remain content with less than that joy which is worth a broken heart.

2. FORGIVENESS AND CREATIVITY

Easily, all too easily, we resign ourselves to the extinction of the creative fire within us. (And that fire is in all of us, whether we are gifted or not – or rather: we are all 'gifted'.) We may look back nostalgically to the time of childhood and youth, when the world seemed to be ours for the asking. Yet the crepuscular wisdom prevails and persuades us to treat the hunger for life as an illusion and the expectation of death as realism. We slip into a purely aesthetic enjoyment of the gifts of culture – the fruits of agonized wrestlings of great men with the meaning of life and death – or we let go of any pretence of creative activity or participation and become content to be entertained, diverted, fragmented. In this we are powerfully aided and abetted by the universal tendencies of our age, by its newspapers, journals, digests, its films and television serials, its sensationalizing of the trivial, the purely informative, by the ease with which it turns the rare experience into something easily repeatable. – We have given up the hope of becoming a promise to our neighbour, and think it naïve to expect him to become a promise to us. (Democracy has not been an undiluted blessing. By instilling in us the assumption that all men are equal – rather than unique – it has often given us no more than the implicit conviction that all men are equally hopeless – as hopeless as we ourselves. Notice the success of writers like S. Beckett, G. Greene, Ionesco.) We are satisfied with knowing no more about our neighbour than can be ascertained statistically. We are ready to do anything that passes the time, as if the passing of time did not most radically put in question everything we are and hope to become.

Forgiveness insists that I was right when I expected the world from my friend and that my friend has a right to expect it from me – for in each of us, and this is our uniqueness, the world is recreated and wants to find expression. I may not be a Shakespeare, a Rembrandt or a Bach, but I am a man for whom the great ones are a parable, a challenge and a promise. The objective world of Shakespeare was not so different from mine, but look what he made of it, how he transmuted it into song, drama, immortal symbols. Bach's world was certainly more uncomfortable and restricted than ours, yet listen how he transfigured it into the promise of eternity. I, too, am called upon by the promise of forgiveness to absorb the world and communicate it to others, instinct with the peculiar flavour only I can give to it. I express my hope in the promise of life by my willingness to be broken in my efforts to reach beyond myself, rather than to remain content with the achievement of that which is within my power.

3. FORGIVENESS IN THE CITY

In politics, economics and the other spheres of our wider responsibilities, we are most easily tempted to discount the promise of forgiveness as irrelevant. In our eagerness to be hard-headed, realistic, down-to-earth, we mistake means for ends, methods for purpose, sheer movement for direction, going anywhere for going somewhere. Here success seems to count for more than faithfulness – a thing done more than a thing hoped for. Yet we ought to consider that it is precisely our worship of efficiency, our implicit acceptance of the ways of power, our trust in success, that have landed and stranded us in the present situation: We find ourselves entrenched in the most intense and unreasonable ideological and economic conflicts, while relying for the defence of our 'unlife' on the ultimate 'deterrent'. We have lost our bearings. We are haunted in the midst of plenty by a paralyzing spiritual vacuity and lethargy. The vast empty spaces discovered by astronomy seem to have entered our hearts and minds. We feel ourselves surrounded by nothingness and our precarious – though often most impressive – achievements are at the mercy of forces that might easily add our world to the general nothingness.

Leadership tends to go to the tough, the unimaginative, the insensitive, to men whose limited and yet limitless ambition is their universe. The masses are fascinated by their empty leaders – dictators, film stars, TV personalities – because modern man needs someone to live his life for him. People clamour for more and more things, more and more excitement, more and more of that security which increases their sense of insecurity. – Do we really hope that we can give a new hope, a new impetus to this world of ours by pushing it a step further along its present path – or by dragging it back an inch or two?

Here more than in any other sphere of human activity, the cross as the challenge of our final forgiveness, could be our hope. To be relieved of the necessity to count one's successes, converts or votes, to be freed from the exclusive domination of the measurable; that is the hopefulness of the cross. In the political and social life forgiveness is the readiness to take risks, the willingness to fail sincerely rather than succeed at the price of sincerity. (It is insincere to cling to a truth of yesterday, to a formula – for the sake of unity, or tolerance, or peace of mind; to affirm that I have understood; to deny the nagging of experience and the harrowing of doubts; to be afraid of changing one's mind, to be thought a turncoat; to hesitate to 'go further' simply because one has already 'gone too far'; to hand one's responsibility over to tradition, a party, a church, a majority: to say or think: 'let us be humble, we are only modest, ordinary men'; or 'how can we remain in power, unless we stick to our programme?') Forgiveness is the chance to renounce any kind of power which has to be bought at the price of freezing our original aspirations. It is the expression of the hope that our sincerity bears witness to a 'truth' that can look after itself – that a 'truth' which needs us as its defenders is not worth fighting for. We exercise the freedom of forgiveness when we are convinced that the innate authority of a sincere word is more powerful than an insincerity backed by the might of a party, a propaganda machine, an army or a church, and when, being thus convinced, we *speak the word.*

Notes

CHAPTER ONE
CLARIFICATIONS

1. 2 Corinthians iii, 4–6.
2. John vii, 45–49.
3. Luke xi, 9–10. cf.: 'Now that you say, "We see", your guilt remains.' John ix, 41.
4. 'Now we know,' say the disciples. 'Now you will be scattered,' answers Jesus. John xvi, 30–32.
5. John xiv, 28; and xv, 5: 'Apart from me' – i.e., our neighbour – 'you can do nothing.' etc.
6. Mark viii, 35–36. Luke xii, 16–20.
7. 1 Corinthians xv, 55.
8. John xx, 21.
9. 'Leave the dead to bury their own dead.' Luke ix, 60.
10. Mark ix, 31. John xvi, 7–11! (The spirit of Jesus – which cannot 'inspire' us, until we see his completed, 'glorified', 'uplifted' life' – will reveal to us the depth and height of our human situation. It will convince us of Jesus' inspiration, and our failure to let ourselves be equally inspired. It can do this, because Jesus yielded.)
11. Matthew xii, 34!
12. Mark x, 17–21.
13. John xi, 26.
14. John xxi, 15–19; Mark xiv, 27–28; etc.
15. John xvi, 29–33!
16. Luke xiv, 26–33.

CHAPTER TWO
JUSTIFICATION

1. G. M. Hopkins: *Carrion Comfort*.
2. Luke xvi, 1–9.
3. Mark x, 42–45.
4. Acts, i, 8. cf. The adventures of Saul of Tarsus.
5. 'The Son of man will be delivered ... and they will condemn him to death ... and they will mock him and spit upon him, and

scourge him, and kill him; and after three days he will rise.'
Mark x, 33–34.

6. Luke xvii, 10; Matthew x, 26–27; Luke vi, 43–45; Acts 4, 20.
7. Matthew xxvi, 52. (This is not an isolated verse, but the summing up of a vital aspect of Jesus' work and the culmination of the prophetic teaching of Isaiah, Jeremiah, Zechariah, etc.)
8. Luke xii, 16–20.
9. Matthew vi, 25–33.
10. Matthew vi, 19.
11. John xx.
12. See pp. 59ff, 118ff, 113.
13. Mark xiii, 1–2. (Behind this verse and those relating to the downfall of Jerusalem, the Holy City, lies the long Old Testament story of the Israelites' insistence – against all prophetic warnings – to trust in their kings, their walls, horses, armies, allies, etc., which are one by one knocked from under their feet – until, left with no human security, they entered the 'diaspora' to survive all empires.)
14. cf. Jesus' attacks on the 'law', the lawyers and Pharisees and Sadducees, on Temple and synagogue, i.e. on all human attempts to 'impose' meaning on life. See chapter on 'Lawlessness'.
15. Luke xiii, 6–9.
16. Mark xiii, 21; Luke xxi, 25–28.
17. 'I did not come to invite virtuous people, but sinners.' Mark ii, 17 (New English Bible.) Luke vii, 36–49; xviii, 10–14., etc.,
18. Luke vi, 22–23.
19. John vi, 25–35.
20. 1 Corinthians xiii.
21. Matthew vi, 2, 5, 16.
22. Matthew v, 20: Unless our righteousness is greater than that of the righteous ... Matthew xvii, 14–21!!
23. cf. Blake: *A Poison Tree.*
24. Luke vi, 24–26.
25. Luke xii, 4–5.
26. cf. pp. 91ff. Also: 'Lawlessness', the *Second* and *Third Temptation*.
27. John xi, 49–51.
28. Matthew xxiii. (Read the whole chapter in the New English Bible.)

NOTES

CHAPTER THREE
THE PROMISE OF COMMITTAL

1. John i, 5–10.
2. Jeremiah v, 30–31. Also Jeremiah ii, 13.
3. John i, 43–51.
4. Mark x, 21.
5. John xiii, 31–35; xv, 13–14; vi, 68–70, etc., etc.
6. John xiv, 12–14; xxi, 15; Matthew xxv, 31–40. Also: Ask and it shall be given, etc. Luke xi, 5–10.
7. Matthew xviii, 3; etc. (cf. the Legend of Paradise.) Because the disciples had experienced his friendship so intensely, Jesus' promise: 'I will go before you into Galilee' was intensely meaningful.
8. Genesis xiiff.
9. e.g. Jeremiah ii; Ezechiel xvi; Hosea xi.
10. The attempt to divide love into 'eros' and 'agape' has done no good. We simply do not know what is and what is not love, where to draw the dividing line between 'selfish' and 'unselfish' love, between 'lust' and 'condescension'. (see my *Irreligious Reflections*, pp. 108ff.)
11. Luke x, 25–37. (You shall – you will – love him whom you cannot help loving.)
12. Luke vi, 38. (See: 'Promise of the Neighbour'.)
13. Luke x, 38–42.
14. The original connotation of *askeo* was 'training', getting ready for, not getting away from. cf. 1 Corinthians ix, 24–27.
15. Matthew vi, 21.

CHAPTER FOUR
THE PROMISE OF WHOLENESS AND LOVELINESS

1. Does the Old Testament or the New Testament persuade us, because it is 'beautiful' or because it is 'true'? Did Plato exercise such fascination over the whole of Western thought, because he was such a great poet or because he was such a great philosopher?
2. Mark iv, 25. Matthew v, 13–14; 28, 19.
3. Luther says: God is whatever you put your ultimate trust in.
4. John i, 1–14; xv; xvi; especially xiv; 1, 18.
5. Whom we do not know.

6. John v, 25; etc. ('Eternity' in John is synonymous with the 'Kingdom' in the Synoptics – in as far as parables can be synonymous.)

7. John x, 17–18; xii, 31–32; 24–26; xiii, 31–32; iii, 14–15; etc., etc.

8. John v; xiv, 6; vi 44–46; xiv, 9., etc.

9. Mark iv, 33–34. (How little even the Gospel writer understood this can be seen by the naïve addition: 'But privately to his disciples he explained everything'.)

10. 'He that has ears to hear, let him hear!' is the ultimate appeal. It would be tedious to give all the references. Most of the parables are well known – and there are many more: e.g. The kingdom is like a net that catches everything; like girls exceedingly determined to get to the wedding; etc. Yet unless we have ears for them we shall not hear 'though one came back from the dead'.

11. Yeats: *The Second Coming.*

12. T. S. Eliot: *Four Quartets.*

13. 'God or mammon'. This passage follows immediately after that of the birds and flowers, and demonstrates that Jesus – or the Evangelist – knew exactly what he was about: the simple life costs, indeed, no less than everything – just as 'forgiveness' (Matthew v, 25–26), see last chapter.

14. T. S. Eliot: *Four Quartets.*

15. 'Peter said, "Here are we who left everything to become your followers. What will there be for us?" Jesus replied, "I tell you this: there is no one ... who will not receive in *this age* a hundred times as much – houses, brothers and sisters, mothers and children, and land – and persecutions besides; and in the age to come eternal life".' (Matthew xix, 27; Mark 29–30. New English Bible) cf. Mark ii, 31–35.

16. 'It is easier for a camel to pass through the eye of a needle than for a rich man to enter the kingdom.' Mark x, 25.

17. 'I have come to set fire to the earth, and how I wish it were already kindled! I have a baptism to undergo, and how hampered I am until the ordeal is over! Do you suppose I came to establish peace on earth?' (Luke xii, 49–51 and vv. 52–53.) 'Abba, all things are possible to thee; take this cup away from me.' 'My God, why have you forsaken me?' (New English Bible.)

18. John xii, 24. cf. Matthew xxv, 14–30; especially the hope to hear: 'Well done ... I will put you in charge of something big. Come and share your master's delight.' (New English Bible.)

CHAPTER FIVE
THE PROMISE OF THE NEIGHBOUR

1. John xiv, 8–11.
2. 'He came to his own country. He could do no mighty work there ... and marvelled because of their unbelief.' Mark vi, 1–6.
3. Mark iii, 34–35.
4. Luke vi, 41–42.
5. Mark xiv, 3–9. (Here the Woman is contrasted with the disciples, who will forsake him, in John xii with Judas who will betray him.)
6. As to my 'God' – this explains the juxtaposition of the 'Two Commandments' as well as the story of the 'Samaritan' which persuades us to love our neighbour as our 'saviour'.
7. Luke iv, 16–30!
8. John i, 39, 46. Also Mark xi, 28–33: 'By whose authority do you do these things?' Jesus is asked. 'What do you think?' is the essence of his answer.
9. Matthew xi, 25.
10. Luke v, 33–38. (I am convinced that v. 35 is a later accretion.)
11. Luke vii, 36–50.
12. Luke ix, 28–43.
13. Luke xi, 29–30. (Jonah's 'sign' was his preaching, his words. No other 'sign' is given to us: only the words of Jesus. Already the First Evangelist was not satisfied with this. He wanted a 'sign' and added the passage about Jonah's three day sojourn in the fish's belly as an allegory of Jesus' Resurrection. He thereby shows how easily the 'Resurrection' can become the 'sign' Jesus refused to give!)
14. Luke xvi, 19–31.
15. Luke xvii, 20–21. Matthew xviii, 20.
16. *The Good Samaritan.*
17. John ix! (cf. v. 3–4: It was not the man's 'sin' nor the 'sin' of his parents that he was blind. But it is our 'sin' if 'the works of God' are not 'made manifest' in our neighbour, if we do not succeed in making him see us as a neighbour.)
18. Luke viii, 26–33. (The state of our mental hospitals – for example – shows that we have not yet understood.)
19. Luke xii, 51–53.
20. Mark x, 35–45. cf. Luke xxii, 24–29. (See also the chapter on

'Forgiveness', The First Supper.) (All Jesus can promise is that his friends will die like him. Concerning the future beyond that he makes no promises.)

21. Luke vii, 18–23. (We may not appreciate that behind the question of John Baptist lies already the vast disappointment which ultimately made the disciples run away. 'Had Jesus come *only* to enhance life?')

22. Jesus remains a beggar – without a home (Luke ix, 58) – always at the mercy of others.

23. Luke xii, 16–20: 'Now I have everything,' says the rich man. 'Now you have nothing,' says God.

24. Mark iii, 20–30!!

25. Matthew xxiii, 13–15.

26. Romans vii, 7–25.

27. 'You shall be perfect, even as God.' 'My yoke is easy, my burden light.' 'If you have no more faith than a grain of mustard seed . . .' 'Again I tell you this: if two of you agree on earth about anything they ask, it will be done for them.' Etc., etc.

CHAPTER SIX
THE PROMISE OF THE CITY

1. Ezra Pound: Cantos, 45, *With usura*.

2. 'By their fruits you shall know them.'

3. Jung tells us somewhere: If a crocodile attacks three bathing women, civilized man will be satisfied with the statement that one of the three was hurt or killed. Primitive man will want to know: Why this one?

4. 'Sell all you have . . . follow me! He was sad . . . he had many possessions. – How hard it is for the rich . . .'

5. 1 Kings xix, 4–18.

6. Luke xii, 29–31.

7. Luke xii, 25–26.

8. Luke xii, 16–20.

9. Matthew xiii, 45–46.

10. Matthew xiii, 44.

11. Luke xvi, 1–8.

12. Luke ix, 3–5.

13. Mark xiii, 14–16.

14. Luke xiv, 16–24.

15. 1 John iv, 20 (cf. the whole of iv, 7–21.)

16. Luke xxii, 25: 'The kings of the Gentiles exercise lordship ...
    and are called Benefactors.'

17. Luke xxii, 26–27.

18. cf. John viii, 39–47: 'The decision is between God and the
    Devil. Jesus calls the God of the Jews a 'devil', just as in Mark
    iii the Pharisees have called the 'God' of Jesus 'Beelzebub'.
    (See also chapter 'Lawlessness', The Second Temptation.)

19. John xi, 49–52. (Just as we prefer our pork to the healing of the
    poor – Mark v – we prefer our peace to our highest hope: Jesus
    is condemned because he raised Lazarus.)

20. Hebrews xi, 13–16. (Abraham etc. are praised because their
    search for the 'heavenly' city was reflected in their citizenship
    here on earth.)

21. Matthew v, 20.

22. Jeremiah, Hosea, Deutero-Isaiah etc., all look back to the time
    of Moses, and forward in the light of what the Israelites had
    then been looking forward to.

23. *Anti-Dühring*.

24. e.g. 'In the Resurrection there will be no more marriage.'
    Fishermen will be sitting on thrones! (Luke xx, 34–36, 22, 30.)

25. Luke xii, 13–15.

26. 'Who are you?' – 'What do *you* think?' Luke xx, 1–8.

27. John vi, 15.

28. Mark xiii, 7–8.

29. Mark xiii, 1–2.

30. 'O Jerusalem, Jerusalem, the city that murders the prophets
    and stones the messengers sent to her! How often have I
    longed to gather your children, as a hen gathers her brood
    under her wings; but you would not let me. Look, look! there
    is your temple, forsaken by God. And I tell you, you shall never
    see me until the time when you say, "Blessings on him who
    comes in the name of the Lord!"' Luke xiii, 34–35.

31. Matthew v, 14–15.

32. Matthew xviii, 19!!

33. We are the light, salt, city on the hill, the 'sent ones', teachers
    of all nations, etc.

34. Matthew v, 21–48: 'You have heard that it was said to the men
    of old ... But I say to you!' (The Evangelist's cautionary
    verses – 17–19 – which seem to contradict the 'I say to you'
    directly, makes one wonder how many more things Jesus had
    said about the commandments which his friends had been
    afraid to remember.)

35. We are to love our enemies – Luke vi, 32–36 – and how can a society preserve law and order for any length of time without enemies.
36. The camel and the needle's eye, the moths and rust, the treasure and your heart, etc.
37. Everything is there to be given away, perhaps without too much forethought. (Matthew xxv, 31–40; Luke xvi, 1–8.)

CHAPTER SEVEN
THE PROMISE OF LAWLESSNESS

1. I do not want to maintain that civilized man is altogether original in the other spheres of the 'law'. But while civilization tends towards increasing autarchy of the various spheres, primitive man seems to treat them as subdivisions of his religious apprehensions.
2. Acts vii. (The whole of Stephen's speech is interesting. It sounds like the last prophetic recall to the desert – in Greek dress.
3. Luke vi, 29: 30.
4. Matthew v, 25–26. (cf. 1 Corinthians vi, 1–8.)
5. Matthew v, 41–42.
6. John iii, 14–15. (cf. the first Apostolic sermons in Acts.) See chapter 'Forgiveness', The Cross.
7. Blessed are the poor, the hungry, the sorrowful, they that have mercy, the persecuted, etc.
8. Mark x, 1–9: 'What God has joined together, man must not separate.' i.e. Togetherness is our destiny. What to make of it, not how to escape from it, that is the question.
9. Mark xiv, 27–28.
10. John xiii, 34–35.
11. Luke iv, 2–4. (I follow the order of Luke for reasons that will appear in the exposition. For 'Matthew', the Jew, political power was still the greatest temptation. For Luke, the Greek, who has seen through the pretensions of politics, the religious presents itself as the graver threat. – See: A.A.T. Ehrhardt: *Politische Metaphysik von Solon bis Augustin*, Vol. ii, p. 29. – Luke is undoubtedly nearer to us than 'Matthew'.)
12. cf. Isaiah xliv, 12–17. This is the most brilliant marxist analysis of religion as an epiphenomenon of the economic process. It is not only full of marxist ideas, it has Marx's very own invective.

13. John vi.
14. Luke xiv, 16–24.
15. Matthew v, 45.
16. Luke xxii, 15–16. Also John vi.
17. John vi, 48–50.
18. Robert Frost: *Death of the Hired Man.*
19. See not only *The Neighbour,* but also *The Trial, The Burrow, In the Penal Settlement,* etc. Especially *The Metamorphosis.*
20. Mark iii, 31–35.
21. Mark ix, 17–19: 'A man in the crowd spoke up ... "I asked your disciples to cast the demon out, but they failed." Jesus answered, "What an unbelieving and perverse generation! How long shall I be with you? How long must I endure you," ... "Everything is possible to one who has faith."' (New English Bible.)
22. John iv.
23. John i, 43–51.
24. Contrast the 'rich, young man' who was asked to pay with everything for a dream – like Nathanael.
25. Luke iv, 5–8.
26. John xix, 37.
27. '"Tell us", they said, "are you the Messiah? ... The Son of God?" ... He replied, "It is you who say I am." They said, "Need we call further witnesses? We have heard it ourselves from his own lips."' (New English Bible.) 'Their judgement was unanimous; that he was guilty and should be put to death.' (cf. the 'It is you who say I am' with Jesus' question to his disciples, 'Who do men say I am?' followed by the, 'Who do you say I am?' followed, in turn, by the strict order 'not to tell any man'; for 'what Jesus is' cannot be told. Only what he becomes to me when he inspires me – Matthew xvi, 17 – matters, and this is essentially incommunicable. (cf. John iv, 42.)
28. Luke iv, 9–12.
29. As only the word of a man can – as Jonah converted Niniveh, Nathan converted David – no sign, no rising from the dead. Therefore: 'No sign shall be given' – Luke xi, 29–32 – 'to a generation that will not believe unless it sees signs and wonders' – John iv, 47–8 – that does not see a sign in everything given.
30. John xvi, 29–32.
31. Mark vii, 1–8. (We need not listen to one who does not wash his hands, does not believe in our creed, disagrees with us.)

32. It is the 'Golden Calf' which we substitute for the invisible God whose very essence is his invisibility, who has to be re-discovered within us, in the midst of us, again and again.

33. John xviii, 4–9; Mark xiv, 49. cf. the whole of John v.

34. 'If it be possible, remove this cup from me.' 'My God, my God, why hast thou forsaken me.' Therefore, to his disciples: 'You will die like me, more I cannot promise.' Mark x, 38–40. 'You will all be offended.'

35. He never commiserates. He heals. He is indignant at the mere suspicion that he might not be willing to heal. Mark ii, 40–41.

36. His prophecies concerning the temple, Jerusalem; his 'I say to you'. 'Until John, it was the Law and the prophets: since then there is the good news of the kingdom of God, and everyone forces his way in.' Luke xvi, 16. (New English Bible.)

37. Matthew xxiii. (Very powerful in the New English Bible. See how 'Matthew' once again tones down the effect by his intro-ductory caution.) Also Luke xi, 42–52.

38. John v, 19ff; viii, 27–30; 54–55; etc., etc.

39. John xiv, 9–11.

40. John xiv, 12; Luke x, 19; Luke xi, 19–23; Matthew ix, 8.

41. 'I am the Resurrection ... Do you believe it?' 'Who do you think I am?' 'If you continue in my word' – i.e. continue to risk doing what Jesus tempts us to do – 'you will know the truth' – discover whether it is the truth for you – 'and the truth will make you free' – i.e. nothing except that which is true for us, which we have experienced as our truth, can make us free. (Only in the doing we shall know – as we can love only in loving.)

42. There is e.g. no 'more or less' in faith. If we have faith as a grain of mustard seed, it would suffice to move mountains.

43. What had Jesus faith in in Gethsemane and on the cross? In that which contradicted him and his faith. (Of course, if we see the Passion as a prearranged supernatural performance – the sign Jesus did not give – everything becomes clear – and irrele-vant.)

44. With that faith the Syro-Phoenician woman met Jesus and changed him, Mark vii, 24–30; with such passion Jesus went to meet death – and death has never been quite the same since, for those who have caught some of Jesus' passion. On the way to the kingdom – if it is the one Jesus promises and looked for – we cannot be deterred by death. Matthew xvi, 21–23; Luke ix, 20–25. As long as we are willing to limit our desires, our hope,

etc., for fear of death, or shame, or insecurity, we are not Jesus' disciples.

45. John xii, 32; 24; 25; John xvi, 7–11: Only after his death has completed his life, will his friends learn to appreciate it, will they be inspired by it.

46. See Matthew, Mark, Luke, John, Paul, Peter, etc.

CHAPTER EIGHT
FORGIVENESS

1. Psalm 130, 4!
2. Matthew xviii, 23–35; Matthew xxi, 28–32!
3. Matthew ix, 9; Luke xix, 1–10, etc.
4. Matthew xxv, 14–30.
5. Luke vi, 31.
6. The Lord's Prayer.
7. Luke xvi, 1–8.
8. 'I tell you this: no sin, no slander, is beyond forgiveness for men; but whoever slanders the Holy Spirit can never be forgiven; he is guilty of eternal sin.' i.e. Cynicism and resignation is unforgivable. Not to have hope for a murderer is worse than murder.
9. John v, 25.
10. John xx, 21.
11. Luke xvi, 16.
12. cf. Galatians, iii–v; 1 Corinthians xv; Hebrew xi–xii, 4; Romans ix–xi; 2 Corinthians vi, 1–10; etc. Also: Matthew xxiii.
13. John ix, 41; Romans ix–xi.
14. See chapter 'Wholeness and Loveliness', pp. 64–5.
15. See chapter 'Committal', pp. 39ff.
16. 'I have not come to invite virtuous people.' Mark ii, 17.
17. 'He who is forgiven little, loves little.' But also: much is forgiven those that love much. Luke v, 47.
18. Mark ii, 1–12.
19. I use the word 'eschatological' as Bultmann uses it in, e.g. 'Eschatology and History'. It is a synonym of 'teleological' with a vast dose of dynamism injected into it. The 'eschaton' is the 'end' in the sense that it faces us from moment to moment with our 'true end', with the question whether we believe that our life has a 'true end'.
20. Acts iii, 8.

21. Galatians ii, 16.
22. Mark ix, 28.
23. 2 Samuel xv–xviii.
24. Luke xiii, 1–5.
25. Revelation iii, 15–20.
26. 'Greater things than I . . .' 'This kind cannot be driven out by anything but prayer' – i.e. asking for the impossible, which we can do if we have faith like a grain of mustard seed. (Mark ix, 14–29.)
27. Mark ii, 6–7.
28. '"The Son of Man has authority on earth to forgive sin." . . . They were all amazed . . . "We never saw anything like this."' 'They glorified God who had given such authority to men.' Mark ii, 10–12; Matthew ix, 8.
29. Mark ii, 14; Luke v, 1–11; John vi, 68. Also Mark x, 46–52; Luke x, 30–37.
30. Matthew xxv, 31–40. This parable is 'eschatological' not in the sense that at a remote 'last day' we shall be rewarded for charitable actions, but that my ultimate destiny, the shape of my life, will be decided, here and now and without my realizing it, by my spontaneous attitude towards those less fortunate than I. What I give – only what I give, yet that sevenfold, pressed down, shaken together – I shall receive. Only he to whom I become a saviour, will become mine. (See below: The Cross.)
31. i.e. if I am so thrilled with my neighbour – when I see the 'Father' in Jesus – that I cannot keep it to myself. Mark i, 43–45.)
32. John xx, 23. I cannot understand this saying in any other sense than that Jesus makes his disciples completely responsible for the proclamation of his hope, which *is* men's forgiveness. Where the disciple of Jesus does not face men with that hope, their fundamental hopelessness will persist. I cannot believe that Jesus, at the last moment, turned his disciples into 'priests' who can pronounce or refuse to pronounce absolution. (Jesus never made forgiveness dependent on repentance: 'Repent, *for* the kingdom of heaven *is* at hand!' Jesus himself never pronounced absolution. (cf. ch. 'Neighbour'.) I therefore believe that the New English Bible makes a grave theological mistake when it translates John 20, 23b; 'if you pronounce them unforgiven, etc.' Linguistically this translation does not seem to be justified. Whether, of course, the Evangelist

had already understood his message in this way, is another question to which we have not yet the answer. (cf. e.g. Hoskyns and Bultmann ad 10c.)

33. See below.

34. Luke xii, 57–59.

35. We must read the whole of Luke vi, 20–49 – or the Sermon on the Mount – to be shocked into the realization that by his concluding parable Jesus wants us to understand that his 'commandments' are not only this-worldly, but realistic.

36. See pp. 64–5.

37. Just as we can only give what we have received (Matthew x, 8), so Jesus can only share what he himself hopes for. He himself must be forgiven, before he can forgive. That is why he went to be baptized by John Baptist as everybody else. Because his hope was really *hope* – not histrionically disguised gnosis – we may hope to share it. Unfortunately, the dehumanization – or deification – of Jesus started early. Already within the Gospel tradition we see it at work. Matthew – unlike Mark – finds it hard to reconcile Jesus' baptism with his stature. In John he is not being baptized at all. Later dogmatic and pietistic developments have removed him still further. That is why we sometimes find it hard to grasp that what Jesus promises to his listeners is his very own: *his* hope. John xvi, 14!

38. Here I do not want to give any detailed references. The last two paragraphs are based on the accounts of the Last Supper in Mark and Luke, and on John 13–17. See also Luke xxiv, 13–35.

39. Luke xxiii, 18–25.

40. John xix, 1–7.

41. Just as the disciples will not be 'inspired' until Jesus' life is completed (John xvi, 7), so his 'enemies' will not realize his 'glory' until they have done away with him. He will appear to them as on 'clouds of heaven' when – according to their reckoning – it is too late. (They had always built the tombs of the dead prophets!) What irony, what sadness, that we see no 'glory' in the son of man while he is alive.

42. The conceptualizations like 'heaven and hell', 'afterlife' etc. represent our attempts to find the peace which does not pass understanding. Yet by separating the natural and the supernatural, time and eternity, we turn Jesus into a Buddha. For it matters little whether we move towards Nirvana or paradise. It is a movement away from this life into which Jesus calls.

43. John iii, 19; v, 24; xii, 31; etc.

44. For this and the following paragraph see John iii, 1–12.

45. 'You must be born again' he says to a wise old man. 'Unless you become like children,' he says to us, etc.

46. Luke x, 17–20. (In this connexion it is worth while looking at Galatians, Romans, Philippians, Colossians, 1 Corinthians i and xv, 2 Corinthians vi, 1–10; xi, 21–29. There is no one who has realized more profoundly than Paul the fulness of Jesus' offer – even though he sometimes clothed his apprehension of it in terms we find it difficult to accept today.)

47. See Mark xv, 29–32 in the New English Bible.

48. The Kingdom is near, at hand, in the midst of you. See pp. 61ff. Cf. The miracles culminating in the raising of Lazarus.

49. Mark iii, 28.

50. I believe that Luke xxiii, 34 reflects an early, but profound misunderstanding. In his whole 'passion-action' Jesus creates the situation of forgiveness. To make him ask the 'Father' to forgive – as if in spite of what was happening – demonstrates how soon the early church learned to shirk the challenge of forgiveness, by passing the responsibility on to God.

51. In the Resurrection accounts, Jesus appears only to his friends and John sums up their intention in the words: 'Have you believed because you have seen me? Blessed are those who have not seen and yet believe.' John xx, 29.

52. 'Simon, Simon, take heed: Satan has been given leave to sift all of you like wheat; but for you' – who will deny me three times – 'I have prayed that your faith may not fail. And when you have come to yourself, *you must lend strength to your brothers.*'

53. To 'incarnate' is to 'clothe in flesh and blood'; to 'realize' to make real, concrete, actual.

54. The teasing of the empty tomb.

55. 'Leave the dead to bury their own dead; but as for you, go and proclaim the kingdom of God.'

56. Luke xxiv, 5.

57. John xx, 17.

58. John xx, 22. (Jesus breathes on his disciples as Yahweh once breathed his own spirit into Adam.)

59. 'Where two or three ... in my name ... I shall be among them ... to the ends of the earth (or: the close of the age).'

60. John xiv, 28.

61. John xiv, 1–11.

62. Wordsworth: Ode. (As Emerson said: 'I am a better believer, and all serious souls are better believers, in the immortality than we can give grounds for . . . and therefore Wordsworth's "Ode" is the best modern essay on the subject.' *Immortality*.)

63. 'Did we not feel our hearts on fire as he talked with us on the road and explained the scriptures to us?' Luke xxiv, 13–35.

64. John xvi, 16–24.

65. Luke xii, 35–40.

MORE ABOUT PENGUINS
AND PELICANS

Penguin Book News, an attractively illustrated magazine which appears every month, contains details of all the new books issued by Penguins as they are published. Every four months it is supplemented by *Penguins in Print,* which is a complete list of all books published by Penguins which are still available. (There are well over two thousand of these.)

A specimen copy of *Penguin Book News* can be sent to you free on request, and you can become a regular subscriber at 3s. for one year (with the complete lists). Just write to Dept EP, Penguin Books Ltd, Harmondsworth, Middlesex, enclosing a cheque or postal order, and your name will be added to the mailing list.

Some other books published by Penguins are described on the following pages.

Note: *Penguin Book News* and *Penguins in Print* are not available in the U.S.A. or Canada.

THE FUTURE OF
CATHOLIC CHRISTIANITY

Edited by Michael de la Bedoyere

'The book as a whole is unredeemable ... a deplorable publication ... disastrous ... it will attract many readers' – Fr Charles Davis in the *Catholic Herald*.

Despite internal opposition the modernization begun by Pope John proceeds within the Roman Catholic Church. Exploiting the freedom of conscience accorded to individual Catholics by the Vatican Council, the contributors to this volume look into the future of their faith and church. Temperately and constructively they try to foresee a church conceived in the idiom of the twentieth century.

'Certainly worth reading. If the views expressed here are not just the views of a tiny handful, the years ahead may see changes in the Roman communion undreamt of only ten years ago' – P.S. Dawes in the *Church of England Newspaper*.

Michael de la Bedoyere edited and contributed to *Objections to Roman Catholicism,* a companion Pelican book.

NOT FOR SALE IN THE U.S.A.

RADICAL THEOLOGY AND
THE DEATH OF GOD

Thomas J. J. Altizer and William Hamilton

'... God has died in our time, in our history, in our existence.' What does it mean to say that God is dead? Is it any more than a warning against all idols, all divinities fashioned out of human need, human ideologies? Does it perhaps not just mean that 'existence is not an appropriate word to ascribe to God, that therefore he cannot be said to exist, and he is in that sense dead'? It means all this and more.

In this collection Thomas Altizer and William Hamilton provide both an introduction to and an exposition of Radical Theology. The Death-of-God radical theologians have no God, no faith in God, and affirm both the death of God and of all the forms of theism. They attempt to set an atheist point of view within the spectrum of Christian possibilities; their aim being to strive for a whole new way of theological understanding.

NOT FOR SALE IN THE U.S.A. OR CANADA